Gender and Competition

How Men and Women Approach Work and Play Differently

Kathleen J. DeBoer

ISBN: 1-58518-876-X
Library of Congress Control Number: 2003115154
Book layout: Jeanne Hamilton
Cover design: Jennifer Bokelmann

"Life with Matthew: A Story about Women, Coaching, and Kids" (pages 80-85) reprinted from *Coaching Volleyball*, June/July 1989, with permission of the American Volleyball Coaches Association. For more information regarding this professional coaches organization, visit www.avca.org.

Coaches Choice
P.O. Box 1828
Monterey, CA 93942
www.coacheschoice.com

Dedication

For my parents

Acknowledgments

Many people made this book: those who innocently and unwittingly appeared in the stories; those who inspired the writing; those willing to plow through early drafts; those who encouraged and critiqued; and those who edited and published.

All their voices are present in this writing. My thanks to David Bettez, Doug Bruce, Pat Host, Reed Polk, and Evelyn Newton, who said, "You *must* write this;" and to writing advisors James Baker Hall, Patricia Lorenz, Roi Ann Bettez, Pat Neat, and Lee Bowman, who said, "You *must* improve this." My thanks to coaching colleagues Terry Liskevych, Mary Jo Peppler, Mary Wise, and Anson Dorrance, who said, "You *must* publish this;" and to professional colleagues Kathy Lindahl, Lauren Patch, Gene DeFilippo, and Sandy Vivas, who said, "You *must* circulate this." And, finally, thanks to friends Mary Ann Taylor, Cathy DeBuono, Kay Cannon, and Bonnie Smoak, who read the manuscript and said simply, "You *must* persist!"

These people helped make the manuscript, but a manuscript only becomes a book when an editor and a publisher decide it is worthy of their *time*, money, and expertise. A special thanks to my editor/agent, Jim Kestner of Kestner Educational Services, and my publisher, Jim Peterson of Coaches Choice/Healthy Learning. Also, thanks to editorial manager, Kristi Huelsing, who was communicative and responsive in the final weeks of production.

Sincere thanks to those athletes who dared to play for me and those willing to play with me, and to my coworkers, bosses, and clients and friends. I did not ask your permission to write about you, I just did. Some of your names have been changed in these pages but many of you will recognize yourselves and others anyway.

My final thanks to husband, Mark, and soul mate, Cate. You listened to all the theories and suffered through all the drafts. My fragile ego could not take much of your criticism and blessedly you knew that, but without you in my life, this writing does not happen.

Contents

Prologue

On an oppressively hot summer day, two volleyball coaches sat on a wooden bleacher in a balcony overlooking a gym floor. Below them, eight volleyball courts held a hundred high-school-age girls. From their perch, the gym floor resembled a popcorn popper, white volleyballs rebounding in random sequence from different courts.

Both onlookers were college coaches on recruiting trips. They held prospect lists on their laps and pencils in their hands. They watched the play with the sclerotic blankness of people who could no longer see the link between their present activity and their future success. The man was head coach of women's volleyball at the University of Colorado. The woman was head coach at the University of Kentucky.

They were good friends: he, part of a growing cadre of men entering the women's coaching ranks; she, a veteran of ten years. Prior to accepting the women's position at Colorado, he had spent a number of years as an assistant coach with the men's national team. They had worked several clinics together and enjoyed debating each other about training techniques and match strategies.

As they aimlessly scanned the courts for an athlete who would make them pick up their pencil, he said casually, "I consider you a friend. Can I ask you a personal question?" Even with friends, she hated conversations that started this way, but without a ready excuse, she said, "Yeah, I guess so."

"Why aren't women competitive?" he asked in a matter-of-fact tone that assumed he was stating a truth and simply wanted the rationale behind it.

She stiffened. "You're crazy," she bristled. "Women are competitive!"

"No," he countered assuredly as if settling down a child. "Women aren't competitive like men are competitive."

"I can't believe I'm hearing this," she snapped back incredulously. "Women are just as competitive as men and sometimes more so. I don't know what you're talking about."

"I'll tell you then," he said. "Listen to this."

He recounted a poignant memory from his days as an assistant coach with the men's national team. They were playing an important match against Russia, a team that had dominated men's volleyball for many years. On this night, the American team was poised to upset them. A win would announce to the world that the United States was a team to be reckoned with on the international scene.

Late in the fifth game, the American head coach called his final timeout. The contest teetered in the balance. Both teams had battled fiercely for two hours with neither able to gain a sustained advantage. This moment would be the head coach's last chance to impact the outcome.

He made a few tactical adjustments. Then, he turned to the team's best player, a man named Karch, and said in a challenging voice, "It's time for you to step it up. You're our best player; you're one of the best players in the world. Show that now! Win this thing for us."

Karch set his jaw, looked the head coach straight in the eye, and nodded. The other team members huddled closely around Karch and the head coach. They knew this was their chance. They all crowded together, joined hands, and rousingly cheered, "USA!" before returning to the court.

Karch played the rest of the match with unwavering self-confidence and incredible energy. He made a critical defensive save, blocked a much taller opponent, and hit with a viciousness unusual even for him. His aggressiveness and sureness seemed to invigorate the rest of the team. The U.S. team won the match.

The male coach on the bleacher recalled the timeout and the win with a degree of reverence. He considered it a masterful bit of motivation by the head coach and filed it in his mental Roledex for future reference.

Several years later, a head coach himself, he was in a similar situation with his women's intercollegiate team. They had a chance to beat Nebraska, a perennial power. A win would catapult them onto the national scene. The situation was the same—fifth game, close score, final timeout.

The male coach turned to his best player and repeated the words of his mentor: "Susan," he said firmly, "it's time for you to step it up. You're our best player. Tonight, you can prove you're one of the best players in the country. Win this thing for us. Now!"

Susan quickly looked away from him and paled slightly. Puzzled, he increased the intensity of his challenge. "You can make yourself an All-American today, Susan! This is the match that gets it done. Prove it right now!"

Still looking at the floor, Susan said through clenched teeth, "You don't have to put this all on me." Completely bewildered, the coach noticed that everyone on his team looked uneasy. They had physically moved away from each other, expanding the perimeter of his huddle.

Susan thrust out her hand decisively as the circle of her teammates widened. Still looking away, she said pleadingly, "Come on, let's just play."

What he had intended to be the most dramatic timeout of his career ended with a whimper instead of a bang. The team managed a weak and uncoordinated, "Go Buffs," and returned silently to the court.

Susan's play after the timeout was tentative and error-filled. She shanked the first pass into the stands. On the second play, she hit the ball so far out of bounds that only the gym wall stopped its flight. On match point, the male coach's team let a "free ball," a routine play, land on the floor between two players. Point, game, match—Nebraska.

"I've never been so upset in my life," the male coach moaned as he finished the story. "My team didn't even compete. They just gave away the chance of a lifetime." His female colleague could see in his countenance that the telling of the story had re-opened the wound caused by the loss. "Now do you see why I think women are not competitive?" he demanded.

"You're a friend," she said in her most conciliatory tone. "I think I can give you straightforward, honest feedback."

"Yeah, please," he said, leaning toward her.

"You're an idiot!"

"What do you mean?" he protested.

"I don't know exactly," she responded, "but I knew when you were telling me the story that what was said to Karch was not going to work with Susan."

"Why?" he asked.

"I don't know," she said edgily, "but it has nothing to do with their individual competitiveness. I know that."

"Then what?"

"I'm not sure," she said, her mood turning pensive, "but I knew it wouldn't work."

That exchange is the genesis of this book. I was that female coach and I wanted to figure out in my head what my gut told me was true. As I did, I realized it was a truth I had spent a great deal of time fighting, a truth I had denied to my own detriment as both an athlete and a coach. And yet, once it dawned on me, I knew it was a truth I had been living all my life.

1

What I Didn't Want to Know About Gender

Males and females are psychologically different. For most of my life, it seemed that everybody but me already knew this.

My delayed conversion was due in part to me spending much of my youth engaged in male-identified activities: fighting, science, and sports. Further, I spent my early adulthood working in *then*-male-dominated occupations—professional sports, coaching, and athletics administration. My advocacy of sameness was basic ego-preservation—if males and females were essentially alike, then I wasn't such a misfit.

My halting conversion toward becoming a believer in gender uniqueness proved to be a dramatic metamorphosis. In my teens and twenties, I argued vigorously from the viewpoint of an outspoken "sameness" advocate; in my forties, I became known as an "expert on gender differences." (1)

I was a hardcore tomboy; if not exactly a girl who wanted to be a boy, then certainly a girl who wanted to do the things boys did—wrestle, roughhouse, lead the neighborhood gang, and urinate standing up. I hated dresses, playing with dolls, and coloring inside the lines.

When I started school, I fought with my mother about wearing pants. What respectable gang leader wears a skirt, anyway? A persistent ear infection that would somehow go away if I didn't have cold air blowing up my skirt permitted a compromise we could both live with—I could wear pants *under my skirt*.

My first-grade teacher once asked my entire class what we wanted to be when we grew up. I blurted out that I wanted to be what my dad was. The teacher laughed at my answer and said I couldn't be what my dad was because I was a girl, and girls couldn't be ministers. My father was working on his Ph.D. at the time, but was also an ordained minister in a church that did not allow women in the clergy. She asked me to make another choice.

Embarrassed, I bluntly refused. She clucked her tongue and shook her head slowly from side to side. Her twenty years of teaching had exposed her to more than one child who would suffer later for irascibly refusing to accept his or her place in life. Wheeling around as if she were the one who had been affronted, she moved to a more cooperative child.

My parents worried about me, but they did not pressure me to change. My mother ignored the advice of a well-meaning neighbor to encourage me to raise the pitch of my voice so I sounded "more like a girl." My parents rewarded me as much for my As in mathematics as they disciplined me for my Ds in penmanship.

My early adolescence was spent consciously avoiding all things female. I refused to shave my legs, pluck my eyebrows, wear nylons or dresses, or carry my schoolbooks against my chest. I embraced the role of neighborhood bully, traded the chore of ironing for mowing the grass, joined an all-boy astronomy class, and mixed bubbling potions with the chemistry set my parents gave me for Christmas.

In later adolescence, however, I also started to develop a feminine identity. My peer group shifted from my male cousins and neighborhood boys to other girls. I still dressed and carried myself like a boy, but I was profoundly embarrassed when mistaken for one.

I remember my eighth-grade science teacher lecturing on body hair, saying that some humans had eyebrows that were not distinct. Their eyebrow-producing hair follicles extended across the forehead, creating the appearance of one solid brow. The teacher said both sexes displayed the trait, but that it was much more common in males than in females. He cited me as a rare example of a one-brow broad. From that day forward, I hated him, but the stray hairs between my eyebrows escaped tweezing for a few more years.

By high school, I was subtly bargaining for acceptance. I was still a jock, but I recall begging my recalcitrant older sister to help me put curlers in my straight brown hair so it would look more like her beautiful blond curls. I started paying more attention to my clothes, grew my hair longer, got my ears pierced, and amid involuntary tears and voluntary cursing, started plucking the hair between my eyebrows.

By college, I was subconsciously making choices to counterbalance my jock image. Everyone assumed I would major in physical education, the popular jock choice of the day.

During my freshman orientation, an English professor, whose daughter was one of my classmates, asked me about my academic intentions. I told him I wasn't sure. He said he would wager that I could succeed in any major I chose.

Taking his kindly encouragement as a competitive challenge, I chose music, the major widely assumed the most rigorous at the small private college I attended.

Privately, I knew I would never be a diva, and actually, I had no aspirations of ever working in the field of music, but the image of myself as a true Renaissance woman appealed to my fragile psyche.

I dated the star basketball player from the men's team for a couple of months, but lost interest after I discovered that he wanted to date someone who valued his accomplishments as highly as he did. That relationship was a harbinger of things to come. It was my first, but not my only, attempt at a relationship with a person as pathologically competitive as I was.

I thrived on opportunities unavailable to my mother or even most women of my own generation. I was engaged in organized sports by the age of 10. I received financial aid based on my athletic ability during my last two years of college. I traveled much of the United States and parts of the world as a member of various teams. Yet it wasn't enough.

I publicly criticized and finally sued the university that had given me most of my intercollegiate athletics opportunities. Their stingy upgrading of the women's sports programs enraged me. I fought and finally left the church that had sustained my family financially and emotionally because of their reticence to allow women into leadership positions. I devoured feminist literature and could find sexism in every situation and male chauvinism in every exchange. My anger ostracized even my closest friends and familial allies.

Two experiences changed me from an angry victim to a vocal advocate of the differences between the genders. First, I married a man demographically similar to myself—an ex-jock, college-educated preacher's kid. Despite our similarities, I found myself in a communication minefield where I was either causing an explosion or exploding myself. Our conversational rhythms were different, our problem-solving styles worlds apart, and our grasp of each other's vulnerabilities nonexistent. Typically, I individualized our problems, alternately blaming my spouse or myself, until I discovered what most around me already knew: gender-related differences in perspective could explain most of our difficulties.

Second, my peer group changed. When I began coaching collegiate women's volleyball, a career I pursued for 13 years, the ratio of female to male coaches was 80-20. By the time I retired in 1993, the ratio in major college programs was 50-50.

As I developed an expanding group of male peers, I was struck by how often they complained about their players' lack of competitiveness. Their criticism was rarely about a particular player; it was directed at females generally.

The accusation unnerved me. In fact, I found it incomprehensible. I was competitive, the women I had competed with and against were competitive, and the women I coached were competitive. What were these male coaches experiencing that I had been missing all these years?

The examples of non-competitiveness that the male coaches focused on described fissures in relationships that preceded a withdrawal from competitiveness. In light of that sequence of events, their players' responses made perfect sense to me. I was as incredulous to find my colleagues mystified as they were by the behavior itself.

Simultaneously, I started reading. A neighbor gave me Carol Gilligan's book, *In a Different Voice: Psychological Theory and Women's Development*. (2) A friend recommended Deborah Tannen's *You Just Don't Understand: Men and Women in Conversation*. (3) A newspaper review piqued my interest in Sam Keen's *Fire in the Belly: A Book about Men*. (4)

A combination of experience and expertise led me to an epiphany. The theories of Gilligan, Tannen, Keen, and later John Gray (5) and Barbara Kerr (6) provided a framework for analysis that helped solve some of the riddles of my world.

I put my thoughts on paper and sent a draft to a male colleague for review. He was intrigued, but not convinced, so he gave it to his female athletes. They said my analysis was correct and matched their own experiences of the world and competition.

The draft of the paper circulated among male coaches all over the country. One began calling it the "bible" and said he read it before every practice he conducted for his team of teenage girls. The affirmations gave me courage to keep writing.

My marriage and career provoked me to posit theories that explained the situations that had baffled and frustrated me. I began to understand that although I had, by choice, lived most of my life in the archetypal male world, I would never shake the sense of *otherness* that I felt when engaged with men in competitive events. I fashioned a model that explained why men didn't think women were competitive, why women didn't think men were communicative, and why each frequently said of the other, "They just don't get it."

What I never imagined, though, was that my conversion to become a believer in gender differences would save me from myself. Allowing for those differences helped me move from a mindset of anger and distrust to one of empathy and productivity. My first-grade teacher might have called it delayed maturation, feminists might dismiss it as psychological accommodation, but the acknowledgment of biology as at least partial destiny finally gave me peace of mind about myself, my femaleness, and my competitiveness.

Differences

Although a convert, I still approach the discussion of generalized differences with a great deal of trepidation. Stereotypes are dangerous. They have served to pigeonhole both genders. In sports, the stereotype of females as non-competitive has served to excuse lack of commitment by the athletes, pardon underqualified coaching, and justify poor financial support. The stereotype of males as competitive has served to excuse inappropriate conduct by athletes, pardon abusive coaching, and justify financial excesses.

Furthermore, pointing out differences between groups is not "politically correct" in today's environment. We are encouraged to feign blindness, at least publicly, to gender, race, age, attractiveness, and many other factors that distinguish us from one another. Our history of race relations in this country has made us justifiably suspicious of "separate but equal" rhetoric.

In a *USA TODAY* interview, management guru Tom Peters predicts that on the gender front, we may have progressed past this obsession to a more functional and honest method of relating. He says, "Until recently, it was not politically correct to think of women as different. If you said women were equal, then they couldn't be different. The wonderful news is we can now say women are equal and different. And that's a huge and dramatic breakthrough." (7)

Yet speaking or writing about generalizations in behavior still warrants caution. Human behavior follows a large bell curve. Variation within groups is as broad as variation among groups, particularly for gender. The male and female behavioral bell curves overlap significantly (e.g., some females demonstrate more masculine traits, some males more feminine traits).

A female coach approached me after one of my seminars and said, laughing, "Okay, now that you have convinced me that I am a man, tell me again how to relate to my female team?" On the other hand, a male applicant for a women's soccer coaching position told me earnestly, "I am much better suited to coaching women than I am men. The harshness that you need to motivate men is uncomfortable for me. I relate much better to women's ways."

The fact that we can adapt our gender-based behavior to fit specific situations provides proof that our humanness connects us as male and female more than it separates us. My behavior changed gradually yet markedly when I moved from the female-dominated environment of women's volleyball coaching to the male-dominated environment of sports administration. I found myself asking less and directing more, explaining less and ordering more, discussing less and deciding more.

Despite these individual proclivities and situational accommodations, our experience still validates patterns of similarities within each gender. Traits do not exclude either gender, but do appear more frequently in one than the other. Behavior is not *gender-specific* but it is undoubtedly *gender-related*.

This perspective proved hard for me to admit after my self-serving, we-are-all-the-same youth. As a child, I attributed my cutthroat tendencies more to early competitive opportunities than to genes or birth order. I thought I was on the leading edge of a naturally developing androgynous personality rather than a few standard deviations toward the masculine side of the female bell curve.

My athletes were my teachers. When I first started coaching, few women on my team had lifelong competitive histories. It was the late 70's and few programs were offered to middle school girls and almost no teams existed for elementary school girls. Many of them started competing in high school—way too late to develop either elite technique or competitive savvy.

By the time I retired from coaching, though, most athletes I had recruited had competed in organized sports since they were very young. My "lack of competitive opportunities" argument for gender differences began to weaken. Although these women athletes had competed since early childhood, as a group they still responded differently to conflict than male athletes.

These differences clearly have led to gender stereotypes. Dangerous as they may be to individuals on the behavioral fringes, stereotypes do not develop in a vacuum. Even I had to acknowledge a basis in reality.

Though tempted to ignore stereotypic differences, I observed among my coaching colleagues that blindness to differences caused great misunderstanding, frustration, and anger. I referred to one group of male coaches as "the woman haters." They complained incessantly and viciously about the ineptitude of their athletes, always blaming the female gender for each shortcoming.

At the same time, I encountered females with only male role models who were moving into coaching positions. These women intuitively mimicked their male mentors' words and actions and felt completely baffled by the hostile and vindictive reactions this behavior elicited from their female players.

Typically, we fear what we do not understand; we mistrust what is different. To find the information stereotypes contain but avoid their value judgments, Harriet Goldhor Lerner directs us to look at context. In her book *The Dance of Deception*, she says, "In the absence of context, we tend to view particular behaviors as fixed 'traits' or as 'personality characteristics' that exist within us, rather than as part of the dance happening between and among us. ... Context allows us to put .... any behavior into perspective. By broadening our view, we are challenged to take a more complex reality into account, to ask questions (rather than provide answers)... ." (8)

Context allows evaluation without righteousness, permitting us to understand differences without cataloging them as "normative" or "deviant." One of the foundations of this book, this perspective is critical for assessing responses to competitive situations. Traditionally, maleness has been normative and femaleness has been an inferior imitation. To maximize the competitive potential of both genders, we must discard these value judgments and look to a larger social context to explain behavior.

In this book, I will forge ahead with broad generalizations. I will refer to males as if they are a collective group with a singular personality; I will do the same with females. If anyone should know better, it is I—the girl who acted like a boy but didn't want to be mistaken for one. Yet these adolescent experiences undoubtedly shaped my conversion from an advocate of sameness to a believer in differences. As much as I was physically an insider—I could shoot, serve, and jump "like a guy"—I was psychologically an outsider—if you hurt my feelings, I quit.

Gender Cultures

Males and females take different perspectives on the world. The experiences that shape values, the situations that cause fear, and the circumstances that define success stand distinct. Several writers helped synthesize my varied experiences into a framework that made intuitive sense to me.

Nancy Chodorow's work was a start. Her research indicates "nearly universal differences that characterize masculine and feminine personality and roles." At the heart of these differences lies a masculine identity defined by a basic sense of living separate from others as opposed to a feminine identity defined by a basic sense of living connected to others. (9)

If Chodorow is right, each gender approaches competitive situations from vastly different contexts. Girls come to the gym seeking to bond as the means to success; boys battle to achieve the same thing. Women enter a workplace predisposed to connect to achieve goals; men compete to achieve goals. Both want to win and both want results, but they hold markedly different ideas on how to access their aspirations.

Although attachment and separation proclivities are fundamental to gender differences, another piece of the worldview puzzle has a major impact on behavioral differentiation. Males learn to view the world as a hierarchical social order. They highly value independence, learned painfully during differentiation from the mother, as a defining trait of maleness.

By contrast, a web of relationships characterizes the female culture, shaped by imitating the primary caregiver. Views of self link closely to the individual's place in that web. They highly value attachment as a defining element of femaleness.

These disparate assumptions about the nature of reality lead to most of our common gender-related stereotypes. In sports, stereotypes perceive males as competitive, females as social; winning is critical to males, team chemistry to females.

Jannette

Jannette and I have only spoken once since she finished college years ago. Just like our very first exchange, this conversation was pragmatic rather than personal. After a few perfunctory "Hi, how are you?" remarks, she asked the *reason-for-the-call* question, "Will you write me a letter of recommendation?"

Though asked often, I felt honored rather than used and each time complied willingly. You see, Jannette played volleyball for me. I coached her for three years at the University of Kentucky, and those two facts alone bond us forever, even if in a bittersweet way. We hurt each other too much ever to forgive each other completely, but the separation of time, distance, and maturity has helped us appreciate each other more than we ever could when we were together.

Necessity brought us together. My program, and therefore my career, was floundering and Jannette was the player who would save me. Jannette needed a second chance, and more importantly, she needed a sense of belonging. Our mutual vulnerability led us to higher expectations for each other than either of us could possibly meet, which only became clear later.

Out of high school, Jannette had signed with the University of Arizona, a full scholarship to a top 10 program avenging the slight of the lukewarm recruiting she had experienced from her home state universities. She was physically gifted but labeled a "head case." Even programs that she would have improved dramatically avoided her.

After two years at Arizona, however, Jannette was struggling. She and the coach disliked each other intensely; she and the team bickered about training and commitment. No one grieved or even protested when she announced she was leaving.

Jannette's two years of training under an elite coach with several All-American counterparts had improved her already-considerable skills. She was good, and I did not care that she had a reputation as uncoachable. Besides, I prided myself on my ability to coach "head cases." I had been one myself. Those who played with me said I could relate to them; those who coached me said I deserved them. Even though I laughed at their observations, deep down I believed them both.

In late spring, I scheduled a recruiting visit with Jannette and her parents. I could see her father was incredibly overbearing and demanding, but insanely dedicated to his youngest child and only daughter. Her mother appeared weak and retiring, and Jannette treated her with obvious disdain. Jannette had her father's large frame and also his strong personality. She was outspoken, competitive, and headstrong. We liked each other right away.

Of interest to me then and now is that Jannette chose twice to play for a female coach. Even after her tumultuous two years under a woman at Arizona, she picked me.

I really believe Jannette was seeking a female hero, a successful woman role model, someone she could respect and emulate. Her yearning was so strong that she tried again, even after her first attempt had failed miserably.

Jannette was 5'11" and a good jumper; she had a beautiful arm swing and was strong and durable. She served and passed well. Her weakness as a player was her defense; she blocked with disinterested carelessness, and she detested floor defense. She prided herself on her ability to decipher offensive intentions and on her disciplined defensive positioning. She believed that the game could best be played from an upright position, even if that meant letting a ball land on the floor. She refused to wear kneepads, calling them unsightly and unnecessary.

During Jannette's first season on my team, she was barred by NCAA rules from competition due to her status as a transfer student. However, she used the time to improve and grow. She practiced hard, lifted intensely, and vigorously supported a team that floundered haplessly through a terrible season. She was determined to make a new start with both her teammates and me.

In her second season, Jannette became one of our primary attackers. As a team, we were vastly improved, but we still choked in critical matches. We competed well enough to press several ranked teams into a fifth game, but then we always found a way to snatch defeat from the jaws of victory. We would shank a critical pass, hit the winning point out of bounds, or miss a serve when we needed a score.

Jannette broke the little finger on her right hand about halfway through the season. We taped it up and enclosed it with a soft splint as protection against further damage. Despite the pain of hitting a ball with a broken finger, she gamely returned to her position as our primary attacker. Blind to both her pain and the impairment caused by the splint, I pushed Jannette relentlessly. She was one of my best players, our best attacker, and one of our key passers. For us to win big matches, she had to perform. It irritated me intensely that she was always in the middle of our late-match collapses. I remembered *her* defensive lapses, *her* hitting errors, and *her* missed serves.

Jannette's father exacerbated the tension to no small extent by insisting that his daughter was underappreciated by both her teammates and me. He would sit behind our bench and growl encouragement to *only* her. He kept his own statistics so he could prove to me after the match that we were intentionally undercounting her numbers.

To Jannette's credit, she ignored her father better than I did. His constant harping though, did serve to focus my attention on *her* mistakes. The season ended just in time. The stresses of competition had turned our first-year honeymoon into an uneasy struggle of wills.

Jannette stayed on campus over the summer, training incessantly. Her personal goal had always been to be named an All-American during her college career. The upcoming season represented her final chance.

We only had one exchange during the summer, but it was a precursor of things to come. I figured Jannette would be one of our captains. She was a team leader, and I wanted to give her a chance for input. I had worked for a couple of weeks on the tactical patterns I wanted to use in the fall. I felt I had come upon several fairly innovative ideas and was eager for approval. Jannette took one look at the patterns and told me there was no way they would work. Defending myself, I explained to her in detail the thought processes behind each pattern. She listened distractedly, then flippantly repeated her criticism. She told me I had placed her in the rotation next to a teammate she despised and therefore my strategy was doomed.

We began preseason ranked among the nation's top 20, a first for us under my tutelage. About a week into our training, we were practicing a part of our defensive system that required our outside hitter to cover a tipped shot on one side of the court, then recover back to the other side to hit. It was a challenging assignment.

We engaged in a drill in which I stood on a chair simulating the other team's hitter and tipped the ball over our blockers into the middle of the court. When Jannette's turn arrived, she cheated way into the middle of the court, negating the challenge of the drill. Irritated by her insolence, I tipped the ball closer to the opposite sideline, forcing her to go to the floor to retrieve the ball and making recovery to a hitting position almost impossible. Jannette hated this type of "sacrifice your body for the team" shtick. Besides, she saw no sense to any strategy that would take her, our primary hitter, out of attacking position.

After two weak attempts at floor defense, she exploded, "Why are we doing this? It will never work!"

From my chair, I said firmly, "It will work. Quit cheating on the drill." I continued lofting soft shots over the block. Jannette fell on her first try, banging her unprotected knees hard against the floor. She let the next ball drop at her feet. The third ball she kicked across the gym in frustration, muttering, "This is bullshit!"

"That's it!" I snapped. "Get out of the drill!"

"Kathy, this doesn't work!" she protested. "I don't know why we are covering this way. We can practice it all day; it won't work!"

"Get out!" I yelled. "It will work, but you have to be willing to sacrifice, and that may mean putting your butt on the floor."

"Oh, that makes a ton of sense," she said sarcastically. "Put your hitter on the floor so she can't hit. Nobody does it this way! This is a stupid strategy!"

I leaped off my chair. "Get out," I bellowed, losing my control. "I coach this team! We do what I say!"

She picked up her sweats. "You're full of shit!" she hollered as she slammed the gym door behind her.

My freshmen looked as if someone had punched them in the stomach; the other players finished the practice obediently, but the gym sounded like a library. I felt terribly threatened, as if I were battling Jannette for control of the team, with her teammates uncomfortable, yet very interested, observers.

During the opening weekend of our season, we played three unranked opponents. We won all three matches, but I was concerned about our team chemistry. We were aced far too often, usually from a simple lack of communication. More disturbing to me was my team's reaction. They set their teeth and silently exchanged dirty looks with each other. Jannette always made sure she shot one over at me, too.

Remembering our summertime exchange about personalities, I made a few changes in our patterns during practice the next week. From my perspective, the new version was tactically inferior, but I gave in to Jannette's manipulations, fairly sure this battle was unwinnable.

Two weeks into the season, we played a match on the home floor of the number-six-ranked team in the country. Jannette had an All-American day; we won 3-2, and our ranking improved from 19 to 9.

A week later, we traveled west to face two ranked teams. We survived the first night, 3-1, fighting the altitude as much as our opponents. The next night, we faced the number-seven-ranked team. They had a great right-side player who scored at will against our defense. Jannette's poor blocking hurt us as much as her excellent hitting helped us.

A large crowd filled the gym and communication was difficult. I wanted our starters to sit in front of me during timeouts so they could hear my instructions. Jannette took less interest in my instructions than in getting water and a towel. She refused to sit with the others.

Going into game five, we all wore the pressure of achievement. A win on this floor would make us a top five team and vindicate us from those critics who said our upset the previous week was a fluke. My team felt exhausted, and we still had no answer for their devastating right-side attacker.

Our opponent jumped out to an early lead, pounding away with their best hitter. I called a timeout and screamed at Jannette. "Take away the line, damn it! Give our defense a chance!" On the next few plays, Jannette hugged the right sideline even though their setter let the ball die short of the sideline. Their right-side player adjusted to the poor sets, pounding uncontested kills into the middle of our court. After each one, Jannette looked at the bench with that, "I'm just doing what you told me to do" smirk on her face.

I was livid. Here was my best player throwing a match simply to spite me. At 4-12, I called my final timeout. "You are the worst blocker in America!" I exaggerated viciously. "Just line up on the ball, damn it, but take something from the hitter." My voice dripping with sarcasm, I finished with, "Any angle will do at this point."

Miraculously, we rallied. Jannette rotated to the back row, as did their star. Jannette served a couple of aces and passed every ball perfectly to our setter, allowing us to set our middle for easy kills. We got to 13-12 when they called their final timeout.

I wanted to change our defense slightly. Figuring they would set their star, I told my middle to commit to the right side. I needed Jannette to block the line shot. All my starters were sitting in front of me but Jannette. She was at the water cooler refilling her water bottle. "What the hell are you doing?" I raged.

"I need water," she shot back defiantly. "I'm dehydrated and my legs are cramping."

"You've got to be kidding," I said between clenched teeth as the horn sounded and we returned to the court.

We served the first ball out of bounds. They aced us to tie the game, then their right-side player pounded two kills down the line past Jannette. We lost 13-15. I was so angry after the match I stayed out of our team locker room, afraid of what I might say.

We flew home Sunday, practiced poorly Monday, and on Tuesday headed three hours down the road for yet another road match. We were 7-1, ranked tenth in the country, and unbelievably miserable.

Our opponent was a mid-major school, unranked, but thinking giant killer thoughts. Four hundred people filled the usually empty gym. One of their players dated a trombone player, who had convinced several of his section mates and a drummer to attend the match. They took their places right behind our bench and broke into raucous noisiness each time I gathered my team around me.

We had no experience as competitors in this kind of setting. My team had eagerly embraced the underdog role battling intently against our string of higher ranked opponents; now we were the heavy favorite. We were physically far superior, but our opponents played with that nothing-to-lose recklessness that every coach fears.

Our opponent served rockets, acing us repeatedly, regardless of our improved baseline communication. They swung wildly, banging balls off our hands and whiffing shots for kills into the middle of our defense. The non-volleyball crowd, enticed into the gym by the promise of free Big Macs, screamed indiscriminately at both excellence and ineptitude. They won the first game, 15-12.

Between games one and two, the motley pep band blasted a cobbled version of their fight song into our huddle. The JV cheerleading squad took the court in front of our bench, and the men practiced throwing the women in the air and trying to catch them, creating alternating gasps and groans from the audience.

I instructed my starters to sit in the chairs in front of me and the rest of the team to gather around them, hoping to create a mini-oasis amid the chaos. Predictably, Jannette refused. One of her teammates asked her to sit down. She shook her off. One of my assistant coaches grabbed her arm and pulled her toward the bench. She viciously ripped her arm free and seethed, "Leave me alone." I finally turned to her and shouted, "Sit down, damn it, or you're done."

She spit out, "I don't know why this is such a big deal to everyone. I hate to sit down during timeouts; it makes my legs cramp." She remained standing.

I turned my back to her and gave the other five players some instructions. When my team returned to the court, five of them slapped hands and Jannette stood alone. We struggled through the rest of the match, extending it just long enough to allow our upstart opponents to self-destruct and defeat themselves.

In the locker room after the match, one of my assistants confronted Jannette. "The next time you are told to sit down, you sit down." Jannette retorted, "Shut up. I don't have to listen to you, get off my case."

We returned to campus in the middle of the night. As we exited the bus, I told Jannette to meet me in my office at 9:00 a.m. the next morning. I did not have a clear plan. I had never kicked a player off my team, particularly not a good one. I called it "cutting off your nose to spite your face," and was incredulous when others did it. But I knew in Jannette I had met my match. Gifted as she was, she was the "head case" even I could not coach.

Jannette arrived 10 minutes late and slumped into a chair in front of my desk. I got up and closed the door. I slowly returned to my place behind the desk and with barely controlled fury said, "What exactly is your problem?"

She exploded, "My problem? My problem? I'll tell you exactly, I hate you! I hate you more than anyone in the world; you're an incredible bitch!" She began to cry. "You're not what I thought you were," she gasped between sobs. "I came here because I thought you were a great coach. I had so much respect for you; now I just hate you." She buried her face in her hands and wept.

Her anguish melted my anger. Sadly, I felt what was left of the pedestal she had put me on crumble under the weight of my shortcomings. Jannette had wanted and needed a hero. I knew that, and yet I could not deliver. Even as I had basked in her early admiration, I knew it would fade sooner or later. It always did. The mundanity of endless training, the stress of constant togetherness, and the pressure of zero-sum competitions combined to make coaching heroism transient. Although mercilessly predictable, the descent from hero to human was always personally painful for me. I slumped back in my chair, drained by my precipitous fall from grace.

"I can quit or you can kick me off the team," Jannette said flatly. "It doesn't matter to me anymore."

"I don't want that," I said softly, struggling to compose myself. "You are my best player. This is your last year. We need each other to succeed."

"I had such huge plans for this season," she said, tears streaming down her face. "I wanted this year to be so good. Now, I don't even care." We sat in silence for a long time.

"Can you and I find a way not to screw it up?" I asked her finally.

"I don't know," she said, recovering some of her brashness. "You're a control freak. I can't stand listening to you bitch at me anymore."

The fight in me was gone. My voice cracked as I said, "I'll try if you will."

My emotion caught her off-guard and she looked up.

"I will leave you alone. I won't try to change you anymore. I won't try to coach you," I said evenly. "But you must repair your relationship with your teammates and quit undermining me. Think whatever you want to about me as a coach. Hate me if you like, but keep your complaints about me to yourself. I'll do the same. It all depends on how bad you and I want this team to succeed."

"I want this team to succeed," she whispered. "This is a great team."

We parted with a tenuous truce. Our relationship remained icy and strained the rest of the season, but we avoided further screaming incidents and direct confrontations. The two of us marched on parallel tracks through the final two months of the season, committed to the same goal, but never connecting.

We won our conference championship and finished the regular season without another loss. We advanced to the quarterfinals of the NCAA Tournament, finishing the season ranked fifth in the nation with a school-record 31 wins. Our only two losses were the final match of the season and the fateful night in Colorado. Jannette was named an All-American, and I was named Coach of the Year.

The day our awards were announced, Jannette brought me a single red rose. She put one arm around my shoulders and, for a long second, held me close. "I wanted to be the first to say congratulations," she said quietly.

"Congratulations back," I whispered in her ear, returning her embrace. "I'm very proud of you."

Then, without another word, she was gone.

I did not hear from her again until that letter of recommendation request. In writing it, I tried to show her how much I respected and admired her.

Jannette was willing to suppress her deep-seated and twice-dashed yearnings for attachment to pursue a personal goal. She overcame the complete breakdown of our relationship to reach individual excellence. I have met few women who want to win that much.

After I did a presentation on coaching women at a clinic, I was asked by one of the male participants, "Is it necessary for females to overcome their biases about relationships to excel in sports?"

"Not most of the time," I answered. "It is really up to us. We must show female athletes that we care about them as people, not just athletes. If we do that, they will struggle and sacrifice mightily to succeed." Then, thinking of Jannette and me, I added, "But, in some circumstances, yes, we may both have to overcome our biases to excel."

Values and Fears

The metaphorical images of pyramids and nets predispose males and females to a set of values and fears that are distinct. These distinctions are not antithetical, just unique.

Males value autonomy, latitude, and winning. Females value attachment, intimacy, and interdependence. Males fear helplessness. They may be wary of commitment if they see it as a loss of freedom. Females fear rejection, isolation, and abandonment. They equate these conditions with loneliness and failure.

These values and fears dictate different patterns of behavior. The task orientation of males means they bond and form alliances through shared activity; the relationship orientation of females means they bond and form alliances through conversation. These preferences for action versus interaction are most obvious when observing the behavior of single gender groups.

Anson Dorrance, the oft-quoted soccer coach at the University of North Carolina, almost stumbled on this gender difference after switching from coaching the men's team to the women's team. He shares the following story: "I had this guy warm up my [women's] team in the early '80s. He was studying exercise physiology at UNC, and it was unbelievable what he did. The women were in a lather, doing agility stuff—just an incredible warm-up. They were so ready to play, and I was thinking, a gift has been given to me. But a month-and-a-half into the season, our morale was shot. I couldn't put my finger on it. Finally, we went back to our old warm-up: The girls come to the field, put on their shoes for five or ten minutes, and in groups of twos and threes they catch up on their lives. Then they jog around the field and end up in a place out of my earshot, stretching. But they're not really stretching. They're socializing. Our morale returned in two weeks.

"It was a wonderful lesson, a reminder of what's important. Men put their shoes on, they stretch, they play. But our [women's] team socializes at every opportunity, and that's as much a reason for our success as the fitness training we do. That 15 minutes it takes for them to put their shoes on and jog around and stretch is a total waste of time, but it's critical for team-building." (10)

Knowledge of this action/interaction difference matters not only for team-building, but is also crucial to understanding gender-biased preferences in activities. If self-esteem is tied to differentiation from others as in the male world, then activities that tend to separate are preferred, e.g., combative, singular, score-keeping activities. Whereas, if self-esteem is tied to integration with others as in the female world, then activities that tend to connect are preferred, e.g., social, collective, leveling activities.

Outcomes vs. Process

A logical corollary to this perspective is the value placed on outcomes versus process. Outcomes identify winners and losers, demarcate successes and failures. Process is continuous and ongoing; it is a journey rather than a destination. The male worldview tends to value outcome over process; the female worldview tends to value process over outcome.

These disparate predispositions play out every day in gyms and on sport fields. I have observed hundreds of teams in many different sports in both practice and play situations. Invariably in practice settings, female teams spend more time in drill sequences, while their male counterparts spend more time in competition sequences. This habit of repetitive training versus game-like training is observable in teams at both the beginner and the elite levels. Furthermore, the pattern holds true regardless of the gender of the coach choosing and directing the activities.

Popular wisdom among coaches posits that this difference has to do with the respective athleticism and skill development levels of the female and male athletes involved in the training activities. They repeat the stereotype that female athletes do not have the same movement abilities, physical strength, or technical proficiency as their male counterparts and therefore must spend more time in drill sequences to improve in those areas.

However, that hypothesis does not completely explain the preponderance of this gender-related training proclivity at both the beginner and the elite levels. I have observed eight-year-old boys' basketball practices where most of the drills are full-court competitive sequences; and I have watched the Brazilian women's national team, one of the best volleyball teams in the world, spend half of their practice on footwork drills. The boys were clearly beginners with no movement ability, physical strength, or technical proficiency; the Brazilian women were just as clearly one of the most athletic teams ever.

The fact is, the difference is in no small part due to our gender-related focus on outcome versus process. Each group trains harder and therefore more effectively when the practice activities match their collective mindset.

Females generally have a higher tolerance than males for the mundanity of repetitive drills. Their process focus means they pay more attention to the details of particular skills and are more attuned to technical specifics. A drill-based training regimen also allows them to bond with each other and the coach through non-confrontational, method-focused activity. The valuation of process over outcome allows groups of females a synergy of spirit in practice settings rarely available to male groups.

Males, concerned with proving themselves, are more easily distracted during repetitive practice than females. They lose interest in drills and have a harder time than females focusing on the specifics of a skill. The lack of consequence in the activity, the very feature that makes it appealing to females, makes it difficult for males. Males are more enthusiastic and therefore more cooperative in outcome-oriented, competitive sequences similar to those found in game situations.

These respective strengths and weaknesses, however, are reversed in actual contests. The valuation of outcome over process allows groups of males a synergy of intent in competitive settings rarely available to their female counterparts. Females, acutely attuned to method, are more easily distracted during competition than males. The primacy of consequence, the very feature that makes competition appealing to males, makes it difficult for females.

Carol Gilligan's work, entitled *In a Different Voice: Psychological Theory and Women's Development*, provides a "separate but equal" model for analyzing the female experience. In explaining gender-related values and fears, she says, "The images of hierarchy and web … convey different ways of structuring relationships … . [E]ach image marks as dangerous the place which the other defines as safe. … [For males,] the wish to be alone at the top and the consequent fear that others will get too close; [for females,] the wish to be at the center of connection and the consequent fear of being too far out on the edge." (11)

Pragmatically, this difference means males and females enter situations with divergent road maps for how to proceed, and eventually how to succeed. "Alone at the top" implies a certain detachment from personal relationships; it requires a degree of distance from underlings, an aloofness from the daily chaos of the average workplace, and the ability to compartmentalize decision-making and emotion. "The center of connections" implies a certain engagement in personal relationships; it requires a degree of familiarity with underlings, an engrossment in the daily chaos of the average workplace, and the ability to co-mingle decision-making and emotion.

Conversation

Sociolinguist Deborah Tannen reinforces Gilligan's models for behavior with her research on speech patterns. In her book *You Just Don't Understand: Men and Women in Conversation*, Tannen describes male conversations as "… negotiations in which people try to achieve and maintain the upper hand if they can, and protect themselves from others' attempts to put them down and push them around." (12)

Tannen's description of female conversation is " … negotiations for closeness in which people try to seek and give confirmation and support, and to reach consensus. They try to protect themselves from others' attempts to push them away." (13)

For men, then, conversation often presents an opportunity for good-natured sparring. Their exchanges, particularly with each other, are punctuated by teasing; their statements are declarative and sometimes combative. Their stories detail mostly actions with little attention to the subtleties of emotion or feeling. Their problem-solving is direct and objective. Conversation is a way to impart information, a means to accomplish a task, or a way to stake out turf.

Women view conversation as an opportunity to share. Talk is a way to develop relationships; it can bridge the gaps between people and make them feel comfortable. Women's exchanges are full of empathic nuances—nods, smiles, audible pauses—designed to promote interaction. They tell stories as wanderings through a range of related topics all tied by emotions, feelings, observations, and reactions. Their problem-solving is oblique and situational. Conversation is as much a part of "being" as it is of "doing."

The Golf Outing

In 1993, I was promoted to the top fundraising job in our athletics department, a risky move by our athletics director. Like his football and basketball coaches, his fundraiser could not fail. The revenues that sustained the entire department came from these three sources. My gender alone was enough to make his colleagues think he had lost his mind, but coupled with my lack of fundraising experience, the decision to promote me looked insane.

Most financially influential supporters of intercollegiate athletics are still men, many older, well-heeled businessmen. They are complete novices at dealing with women in matters of money, other than an occasional charitable function. These individuals represent critical allies of any major college athletics department because they have both the wherewithal and fervor to help programs succeed. Their gifts build facilities, pay for million-dollar coaching contracts, and provide endowments for scholarships. No athletics administrator would intentionally make this group feel uncomfortable.

To mitigate the supporters' anticipated hesitancies and give me a chance to succeed, the athletics director had his senior associate, a man the supporters all knew, write a letter shortly after I was hired. He told them he would be handling the major donors and invited them to call him on any matters of concern to them. Both he and I knew he had little time for this group and even less interest in fundraising, but it was a gesture meant to smooth the transition.

I came on board in August. By the following spring, I had a lead on a new million-dollar donor. He and another one of our major supporters wanted to spend some time with the athletics director. Both these men had vacation homes in North Carolina and had independently invited the athletics director to come to their turf and play golf. He knew the importance of this type of casual, no-agenda time with supporters, but his many years of travel and recruiting had dampened his enthusiasm for these donor-funded boondoggles. To me, these activities were huge perks—beautiful golf courses, private planes, posh houses, and social time with those who supported our agenda. Of course, these events had traditionally been male-only, so I was at once excited and petrified when I was invited.

The three-day junket was an initiation for me. It was a tryout, a way to see if I could function as "one of the boys." These men were friends in the male sense of the word—they knew a lot about each other's golf games, business pursuits, and politics, little about each other's families and feelings. Golf was a way to spend time together. The men teased each other incessantly, told funny stories about other golf outings, bragged about an accomplishment here and there, and raged about the government or employees or other obstacles to their success.

I wanted very much to fit in and not make anyone in the group uncomfortable. These men did not usually play golf with women, but I hoped my gender would be ignored. We played a game-within-the-game called "pass the trash" in which playing partners and bags rotate to different carts after every six holes, permitting each of us to play six holes as pairs. The mini-game is an excellent way to mitigate ability differences and encourage camaraderie among all participants in a foursome.

My golfing skills were not as good as either the athletics director, who played at a 12 handicap, or the senior associate, who played at an 8. Fortunately, my skills were comparable to those of our hosts. They were both very successful businessmen in their early sixties with homemade swings, poor short games, and extremely competitive natures.

I started playing golf after I finished college. I learned the game by mimicking others and applying an occasional tip from another player or a golf magazine. My playing comrades were always male friends or other women athletes learning golf after successful careers in other sports. More from ignorance than protest, we always played from the white tee boxes—by golf etiquette, the men's tees. Like me, my female counterparts were strong and struck the ball aggressively. Like most male golfers, we struggled more with direction than distance. We enjoyed the challenges and hazards of the golf courses and found the assumption that women could not hit the ball any distance or over a hazard both demeaning and patronizing. We felt we had every right to lose balls in ponds and woods at the same rate as our male counterparts.

As I approached the first tee at the exclusive country club in North Carolina, accompanied by my male bosses and one of our biggest donors, I decided a political protest about the sexist nature of golf course design was not the best way to keep my gender inconspicuous. My decision was confirmed when I realized after several holes that had we been playing from the same tees, I would have outdriven our host on most occasions. Our different starting points allowed them to "ooh" and "aah" about my drives and me to demurely credit my success to the ladies' tee placement.

The shortened course, however, did significantly help my game. On one long par five, I hit the green in two shots and sank a 10-foot putt for an eagle. I was playing with the grand poobah at the time, and my score allowed us to beat my work compatriots, no small feat for two high handicappers. My partner was elated and my worth was established.

We switched partners, bags, and carts at the next hole and after some light-hearted trash talk about who was carrying whom, our host stepped to the tee box and promptly sliced his ball into the woods. He muttered to himself about slowing down his backswing. I volunteered, "You're right, that was one fast draw." The senior associate said to his new partner, "How about that, she gets an eagle and all of the sudden she's giving lessons." As if on cue, I also hit my drive out of bounds.

My golfing skills were ideally suited to this setting. My distance was manly enough to warrant their respect and to prevent arrhythmic play, yet my chipping and putting were bad enough to keep my score a competitive but not threateningly-high number.

For three days, the conversation was male-speak. Even at dinner, after a couple of drinks, our dialog never went beyond golf, our football or men's basketball teams, stories of interactions with other high profile men, or complaints about unreasonable obstacles to even greater successes. This was friendship talk to my male counterparts, acquaintance talk to me. It was pleasant but not bonding. After a while, I realized that was the point.

The outing was a success. Our carefree banter and mutual kidding made our donors feel at ease. One remarked to me later, "I can tell you three really like each other. You're all over each other all the time." Our incessant teasing of one another was his clue to our affinity.

When we returned home, I spent about 30 minutes telling my husband the details he wanted to hear. I told him about the golf courses we had played—describing the holes, layout, and hazards in as much detail as I could remember. I told him how we had played—who won, which day, how they won—and I told him about our hosts—their fortunes, their properties, and their friends.

Then, I called my closest female friend and we talked for two-and-a-half hours. I described my hesitancy about the trip—my desire for inclusion, yet my fear of failing as either a companion or a competitor. I described my colleagues in great detail— analyzing how they interacted, their hang-ups, their politics, and their idiosyncrasies. I described the houses—noting the design, the furniture, the presence or absence of family pictures and who was in them. I also described my gnawing sense of aloneness as the days progressed, my feeling that what was not said was much more important than what was said, and the exhausting impact of the constant teasing. I forgot to tell her about the golf courses or who had won and lost each day.

Learning

In the 1982 book *Women's Ways of Knowing*, the authors develop theories about learning through interviews with females in different stages of their lives. The authors hypothesize that people gain confidence in what they know in two distinct ways—one they call *separate knowing*, the other *connected knowing*.

These different ways of accessing knowledge are not gender-specific in that both males and females utilize each method, but they are gender-related. These researchers posit that, "… more women than men tip toward connected knowing and more men than women toward separate knowing." (14)

Separate knowing is the method most often used in traditional educational settings. It is book learning. Value is placed on objective review and analysis. The student is convinced something is true by the evidence accumulated to prove it.

Connected knowing is show-and-tell. Value is placed on the learner's ability to correlate situations and experiences. The student accepts something as true because they have experienced it or can conceptualize a situation similar to it.

My early struggles with my own gender identity and my advocacy of gender uniformity resulted in part from the incongruity in what I was told was true (separate knowing) and what I experienced as true (connected knowing). The arguments of adults did not jibe with my childhood reality.

Their message was that boys and girls were different; yet my experience was that I had more in common with my male cousins than I did with my older sister. Their statistics said that girls were better at reading than mathematics; yet I could never graduate from the slow reading group and got the only A+ of my elementary school career in arithmetic. Their conventional wisdom held that boys were stronger than girls; yet my dominance of the playground gang attained by upending and sitting on anyone who challenged me made that message dubious. In my links to the world—family, school, friends—I felt more connected to the opposite gender than to my own.

Arm Wrestling

One of my most memorable childhood moments occurred when I was 13. I was in an eighth-grade class with the biggest, strongest boy in the school. We attended a parochial school with a largely Dutch, Protestant constituency. He was one of only three African-American students in the school, and the only one in the junior high. He was taller and more muscular than most of the other boys, and I sensed they were a little afraid of him.

We were kidding around in a break period between classes one day when he challenged me to an arm-wrestling duel. When I surprised him by accepting, he quickly moved his chair to the opposite side of my desk, rolled up his sleeve, and, looking around for an audience, prepared for a quick victory. We carefully positioned our right elbows on the table and gripped hands; then we locked our left hands together in between. He chuckled good-naturedly, humored by my feistiness. Together we counted, "Three, two, one," and began our desktop combat.

Neither one of us could gain an advantage for an amazingly long period of time. The improbable nature of our duel—a white girl arm wrestling a black boy—and the even more incredulous stalemate drew a small crowd of classmates. We were both straining, our jaws set, our heads bowed, shuffling our feet under the desk in a futile attempt to gain leverage. It never occurred to either of us that we would lose this contest.

Finally, I felt his arm weaken almost imperceptibly. My shoulder ached all the way into my lower back. Try as I might, I could not push any harder on his arm, but in an attempt to seize a psychological advantage, I intensified my grip on his right hand. Both of us were sweating and had started breathing in short shallow gasps. He was strong enough and competitive enough to resist my pressure even as his arm bent awkwardly backward. Only when the back of his hand finally touched the desktop did he relax in defeat.

My 13-year-old identity was closely tied to my athletic prowess, and I was really quite proud of my victory. However, my concern for his feelings dictated that I did not gloat or celebrate the result. At that moment, the fact that my physical competence would one day be viewed as a liability in forming relationships with men held no significance for me. Even if it had dawned on me, I would not have cared. My feeling at the time was that boys and girls were pretty much the same. My success at arm wrestling did not have a political context. It was a simple truth: in a contest of equals, I had won.

Achievement vs. Conformity

These distinct ways of learning—separate knowing and connected knowing—predispose us to unique developmental paths. In the male paradigm, acceptance is earned through performance. In the female paradigm, by contrast, acceptance is a prerequisite to performance.

When Carol Quit

I remember arguing desperately and vainly with one of my best friends named Carol after she told me she was quitting our high school basketball team just before her junior year. She had had a great sophomore season and would have been one of the stars on our team.

Carol told me her parents said she needed to get a job. I asked why her brother, a relatively average swimmer, did not have to quit to get a job. She said her brother had aspirations of swimming in college and the family wanted to encourage those dreams. I argued that, with her skills, she had a much better chance of competing in college than her brother did. Carol responded that it was time for her to quit sports and that the job was not only her parents' wishes but hers also. She wanted more time for social activities, a boyfriend, and more money for clothes.

I was both angry and hurt. Carol's assumption that accomplishment in sports was not compatible with acceptance in high school was deeply threatening to me. I felt rejected and abandoned. We spent little time together after she quit, both finding new peer groups.

I realize now that we were acting out a very common script for adolescent girls. Barbara Kerr, in her book *Smart Girls, Gifted Women*, says adolescence is the time girls struggle most with issues of "conformity versus achievement." She notes, "It is likely that society's emphasis on the impossibility of combining love and achievement forces many gifted girls to become preoccupied with their relationships rather than personal achievement." (15) The quest for identity is for most girls, like my friend, rooted in belonging and approval rather than, like her brother, struggle and performance.

Competitive Behavior

The gender-differentiated links between acceptance, struggle, and performance are essential keys to understanding competitive behavior. To excel, whether in athletics or other challenging endeavors, people must be convinced to struggle. The link between struggle and performance is gender-neutral—*all* must struggle to achieve.

Where gender enters the equation is in the relationship of acceptance to struggle and, therefore, transitively to performance. Females need to feel acceptance before they will commit to struggle. Males will struggle first, expecting acceptance only after they perform.

Female Acceptance—Struggle—Performance

Male Struggle—Performance—Acceptance

This gender difference is obvious in the play of children. When a group of boys allows a younger child to join them in an athletic activity, the youngster is granted no special consideration. The boys will play at their own skill level, and it is up to the younger child to keep up, drop out, or be kicked out. When a group of girls engage in an athletic activity with a younger child, they will modify the game so the youngster has a chance to succeed. (16)

Breakthroughs

A friend of mine used to coach both male and female cross-country teams at a major university. In his observation, the groups responded differently to a time breakthrough by a particular runner.

On the men's team, when one of the runners dramatically reduced his time, several others were likely to experience a similar surge after a period of training. The breakthrough of one runner served to motivate his teammates—he showed them possibilities, made them fear falling behind, and challenged them to push harder. When team chemistry was good, the excelling runner always became the "leader of the pack." His performance earned him acceptance, status, and respect. The positive team chemistry created validation and support for others in the group. They drove themselves to perform, often lowering their times.

With his women's teams, when one runner excelled, the other runners reacted differently. They teased her by calling her the coach's pet; they said she was trying to make the rest of them look bad, and that she wanted to be the star. Privately, they also often expressed discouragement with their own performance.

In the women's group, the breakthrough caused a tear in the comfortableness of the relationship web of the team. By taunting her, the others separated themselves from the excelling runner. While the male star, through his achievement, became the leader of the group, the female star was made an outsider. Instead of being rewarded for achievement, she was punished.

In reaction to this punishment, the breakthrough runner on the women's team often worked hard to win back the favor of her teammates. She effusively encouraged their efforts. She bragged about them in public, always giving credit for her good showing to their efforts. Sometimes, she even slowed herself slightly in training, running just at the head of the group, as if pulling them along.

When team chemistry was good, this behavior had a significant impact on the performance of the group. My friend observed that when his female runners ran as a pack, the individuals put tremendous pressure on themselves to "do their part." They drove themselves to personal bests in their quest to stay with the team and not disappoint their teammates.

Both genders derived self-esteem from the same activity—running as part of a team—but the source of their reinforcement was different. The males achieved their sense of self from their position in the hierarchy, the females from their position in the web. For the males, standing was determined by what they did and how well they did it—performance. It was only peripherally associated with their ability to connect and maintain relationships. For the females, standing was determined by their ability to connect and maintain relationships—acceptance. It was only peripherally associated with what they did and how well they did it—performance.

Hence, male runners pushed themselves to catch a colleague who had outdistanced them. Struggle preceded acceptance in the group. Female runners pushed themselves to fulfill their obligation to the group. Acceptance in the group preceded struggle. In both cases, the performance of the group was enhanced by the accomplishments of an individual runner even though their personal motivations were different. In both cases, the ability of the "star" to connect with teammates magnified the impact of the individual achievement. My friend's best teams had both individual stars and good chemistry.

Cross-Gender Settings

The dynamics of same-gender competition are exaggerated in cross-gender settings. Men are more wary of the penalties for failure when competing with women, and women more wary of the penalties for success when competing with men.

Tennis with the Boss

Early in my coaching career, I played quite a bit of recreational tennis. The athletics director who had hired me at a Midwestern university was an avid tennis player. We both played in a lunchtime doubles group. I was the only woman, but had been invited to join when it was clear my skills were sufficient to add to the competitiveness of the group.

One day, none of the other players showed up. The athletics director and I hit back and forth for awhile, waiting anxiously. When it became clear no one else was coming, he suggested we play singles.

I killed him.

Unlike my adolescent arm-wrestling victory, at 26, I felt very unsettled about this conquest. I was glad I had won, but I wanted no part of further competition with my male boss. A day later, he asked me to play singles again. I made up an excuse to dodge his challenge. He persisted, asking me daily for a rematch.

A week after our first duel, we played again. I was anxious and unfocused. I struggled mightily with my serve, the best part of my game, double faulting countless times. He beat me 6-4, 6-3. I was angry at myself for my lack of competitiveness, but also, at a complete loss to explain my sudden ineptitude.

We never played singles again. Nor, to my knowledge, did either of us ever mention our duels to anyone else. What had started as an innocent quest for a game to fill a lunch hour became an uncomfortable struggle that involved much more than just tennis. We had naively stumbled into the dangerous territory of our respective gender socializations.

The voice of his socialization mockingly screamed at him, "You lost to a girl?" The voice of my socialization unnervingly chided me, "Winning is not necessarily better than losing if someone gets hurt in the process."

John Gray speaks of these competitive role stereotypes in his book *Men are from Mars, Women are from Venus*. He says women learn a "lose/win philosophy—'I'll lose so that you can win.'" (17) Men learn a win/lose philosophy—I want to win, and I don't care if you lose. (18) His book urges a re-evaluation of these social contracts, highlighting their incompatibility with long-term heterosexual relationships. But his identification of these divergent maxims as one of the psychological underpinnings of male/female attraction explains the anxiety endemic to cross-gender competitive events.

Neither the athletics director nor I had a relationship agenda beyond our work roles. We liked and respected each other, but we did not flirt, were not physically attracted to each other, and were each romantically involved with other people. We worked together, and, at times, played together. Yet even our wholly platonic relationship was not immune from the subconscious shadows of gender socialization.

Mano a Mano

John, a philosophy professor, Vietnam war veteran, and part-time housemate from my post-college days, provides a first-hand account of the male perspective on cross-gender competition.

In the late '70s, we were both training under the tutelage of a mutual friend and track coach, Mike, who also owned the house we shared. I was preparing for my second season of professional basketball; John was trying to recapture the fitness level he had enjoyed as a college wrestler. Mike had designed individual, yet similar, workouts for each of us and was fond of posting our times on the refrigerator door. On the track, running gut-wrenching repeat 440s, John and I were relatively equal. Knowing the benefits of a training partner, Mike occasionally invited John to join me for a workout, an offer he accepted, but always found a way to avoid.

In an article about those days that he wrote several years later, John said, "I have long advocated sexual equality, and I have usually managed to practice what I preach. But when it came to equality on the playing field, I came up short. I had never felt so threatened." In analyzing his apprehension, he states,

> "… there was more to my reluctance to do battle with Kathy than the fact that we were equals … . She was the type of woman I sought as a mate. And that made a difference.
>
> "Had I lost to Kathy, would I still have had something to offer her? Women like Kathy don't need men for the conventional reasons. They are capable of being good providers … . They are more interested in becoming doctors, lawyers, or professors than in marrying one. In short, I could not count on my income or my intellect to underwrite my manhood.
>
> "Besides, is not a real man one who can lay it on the line physically …? Could Kathy be attracted to a man who had shown less grit than she? More importantly, could I feel secure offering warmth and laughter to a woman who was tougher than I?"

In discussing his current relationship, John said, "I am happily engaged to a woman who is a very fine athlete. … Yet … Anne and I have never competed in a way that might reveal who is made of sterner stuff, and the thought of going *mano a mano* with her is disquieting."

John's candor is enlightening. He clearly identifies the subtle dangers in cross-gender competition—the very *stuff* that drives success in competitive situations, the sterner stuff, as John calls it, is also the *stuff* that compromises intimacy in relationships. (19)

Psychological Adjustment

Barbara Kerr's *Smart Girls, Gifted Women* attempts to explain the differences in achievement levels between the gifted girls and boys who were her classmates in the late 1950s and 1960s. They were all part of a post-Sputnik accelerated curriculum designed to produce the "Leaders of Tomorrow." The idea for her book was conceived at the 10-year reunion of her high school class in 1979, when she noted that the professional achievement levels of her female classmates were significantly lower than those of her male classmates.

In her chapter entitled "Barriers to Achievement" Kerr observes: "… there is [an] internal barrier to achievement that ironically is not related to any unhealthy psychological state, even though it, too, often results in underachievement. It combines a healthy psychological state with an accommodating personality. This barrier is psychological adjustment, the process of resourceful adaptation to the environment—compromising and adjusting in order to survive and to cope psychologically." (20)

Like Elisabeth Kübler-Ross before her, Kerr lists the stages of adaptation experienced by those who must cope with an uncontrollable catastrophe. Denial is the first step in the very predictable process. It is followed by bargaining—making a few minor adaptations, anticipating that the familiar routine will resume. The next phase is anger—rage over the unfairness of the situation. Finally, the process resolves with acceptance—mental and physical adjustment to the new situation. (21) Kerr equates the experience of femaleness in historically male-defined domains to the experience of those dealing with a life-changing catastrophe.

I can track my progress through all these stages and my intermittent return to each of them. As a young child, I flatly denied that any differences existed between boys and me. I capably competed with them, ignoring the taunts of "tomboy" and chastisements for "unladylike" behavior. By adolescence, I was bargaining. I knew we were different and had stopped coveting maleness, but I still assumed that our differences were subtle and inconsequential and certainly would never affect my future.

Anger ruled much of my college and professional athletics career as I eagerly jumped on the feminist bandwagon and fought the status quo. I left the church, sued the university, ostracized my family, and righteously attacked everything and everyone.

Acceptance came late and slowly. The realities of getting, keeping, and succeeding in a job forced pragmatism into my viewpoint. The responsibility for problem-solving, a task vastly more challenging than problem identification, tested my simplistic solutions. Marriage and, later, discussions about children and aging made me confront my own choices. Now, at middle age and finally comfortable with my identity, I accept and can celebrate gender difference as one of many facts that has shaped my life.

Rather than the barrier to achievement asserted by Kerr, I prefer to think of psychological adjustment as a necessary step towards taking responsibility for one's own choices. Acknowledgment of choices in the context of gender differences can present opportunities to examine relationships from the perspective of "the other." And, the realization that no one, male or female, can "have it all at the same time" is a liberating epiphany.

2

Gender Differences in Competitive Play

In 1973, one in nine girls played high school sports (11%); 25 years later, in 1998, the number was one in three (33%). (1) This single statistic reflects a massive social change in our culture.

Sport is a mirror of societal values. The games we play and who gets to play them reflect our attitudes and ambitions. Historically, athletic participation was part of the male rite of passage from boyhood to manhood. Today, participation in sport is seen as a necessary component in a well-rounded childhood. The gender specificity is gone. Sport is valued as part of the transition from childhood to adulthood.

In an article in the *New York Times* Sunday edition, Anna Seaton Huntington noted that this attitudinal change had reached all the way to Miss Porter's School, an elite all-girls preparatory school in Farmington, Connecticut.

As Huntington observed, the school "has long held to a tradition of emphasizing courteous recreation and participation rather than winning on its athletic fields." One of the students commented, "There was this attitude of: 'Oh, we're Miss Porter's. If we lose, that's O.K. ...'"

Observes Huntington, "That one of the oldest girls' schools in this country is pushing to shed its image of white gloves and cotillions in favor of softball mitts and basketball games reflects a broader change in the culture of girls' and women's sports from a focus on politeness to competitiveness, and may signal a fundamental change in what it means to educate a girl in this country."

In the article, M. Burch Tracy Ford, the head of the school, asserts, "... for girls to really be successful, in their personal lives, in a business or political context, or any other venue, they have to learn from boys and men about exercising their strength and power, and sports are a perfect vehicle for teaching that." (2)

For females, the change from supporter to competitor has not been seamless. Competition involves a paradigm shift. Competing identifies who is one-up and one-down, who is ahead and who is behind, who is winning and who is losing. This separation of others into tiered groupings is uncomfortable for most women. For females, life is more like an extended family reunion than a contest.

A junior high physical education teacher shared the following story. He had been teaching eighth graders to play volleyball in gym class for twenty years, and the pattern of interaction never changed. The first day of the volleyball unit, he would set up the nets and leave the balls on racks in the corner of the gym. The first boy to enter the gym would grab a ball. He would kick it, dribble it, or throw it against the wall until another boy came out. Then, within two minutes, they were on opposite sides of the net, engaged in a game. As more boys entered the gym, they either joined the game or went to another net and started their own game.

The first girl to enter the gym would take a seat on the bleacher and wait for her friends. As more girls came out of the locker room, they would visit in groups around the edges of the gym. After several minutes of visiting, they would take a ball, form a circle of four to six, and pass the ball around the group, laughing and talking the entire time. These different activities, chosen independently, one competitive and one social, would last until the teacher called the class to order.

The Importance of Winning

Our hierarchy and web perspectives affect attitudes towards competition in a variety of ways. None is more obvious and fundamental than the difference in attitudes toward "winning."

In males, the importance of winning is largely unquestioned and unchallenged. Vince Lombardi's oft-quoted statement that "winning isn't everything, it's the only thing" typifies the male mindset. The assumption that winning is primary is so universal in the male world that it is viewed as natural and normal.

In females, winning is only one among several options. Women will evaluate the costs of winning in relation to the other options. If the costs are too high, particularly in the area of interpersonal relationships, then winning will lose significance.

Angela and Cathy

Sometimes, when coaching volleyball, I lost sight of the mindset I shared with the women under my tutelage. I was particularly fond of a drill that pitted one athlete against another in an exhausting struggle to score a certain number of points. One day, I put my starting middle blockers, Angela and Cathy, against each other in this drill. They were roommates and good friends.

On this particular day, Angela was uncharacteristically non-competitive—her efforts lethargic, her resistance inept, and her usual aggressiveness non-existent. Her ineffectiveness frustrated me and her lethargy angered me. The longer the drill went on, the more agitated I became. In an effort to motivate her, I hollered, "Angela, are you going to compete or not? She is killing you! Don't you want to win? What kind of an effort is this? Where is your pride?"

Despite my scolding, Angela's performance and effort declined still further. Exasperated, I finally stopped the drill and asked her, "What's the deal with you anyway?" She looked me squarely in the eye and said, "I don't care if she beats me. I don't need to win; she's my friend."

I assumed that winning the drill was Angela's primary motivation. My challenges to her were driven by that supposition. Her friend and opponent, Cathy, was a good player, and the pied piper on our team. Everyone wanted to be her friend. Angela had no urge to beat her or to win the drill for winning's sake.

My failure to grasp her mindset resulted in completely inappropriate communication. What likely would have motivated Angela were admonitions that her lack of effort was hindering her friend's progress. I should have hollered, "Angela, isn't Cathy your friend? Don't you care about her? How can her skills improve if you don't challenge her? You must make each other better if we are to succeed!" This appeal to guilt was much more in harmony with Angela's worldview. I needed to convince her that competing with Cathy would strengthen their connection, not diminish it.

Females not only evaluate the costs of winning, but also have different standards for measuring the benefits of success. They do not tacitly assume that winning is worth the sacrifice required. Women's culture ties self-esteem to connectedness as much as to achievement.

An Associated Press article reprinted in the sports section of a local newspaper provided a clear example of this perspective. The article, entitled "Running From Stardom," told of 17-year-old Amani Terrell, a high school track star with Olympic potential who decided not to run in college. In describing Terrell, the writer says, "… she realizes that running at the next level would take from her the one thing she really wants: a life. … She has had enough of the grueling practices and competition that consume the lives of so many young runners and other female athletes, such as gymnasts." Terrell is quoted as saying, "I want to have friends, a boyfriend. … I don't want track to be my whole life … ." (3)

For this young woman, the benefits of winning did not outweigh the sacrifices required. She and the writer shared the assumption that, for females, "a life," "friends," and "a boyfriend" were not compatible with the pursuit of high level competitive achievement.

Tony

After I finished college in 1978, I was drafted by a start-up women's professional basketball league. The Women's Basketball League (WBL) was one of the first attempts to make women's basketball into a profitable venture. From my perspective twenty years later, there is little reason to believe the league had a chance to succeed. Women's basketball was still in its infancy on the college level and few programs were drawing significant crowds, much less making a profit. Network television still dominated the market and little advertising money chased women's team sport programming.

Oblivious to these obstacles, I readily signed on. The offer of $150 a game astounded me, especially when I realized it added up to $5,000 for the season. That was more money than I had ever had, much less thought I could earn playing the game that I loved.

I had much to learn about sport as a business. I certainly understood the link between winning and success, but I was naive to the link in professional sports between winning and survival. Our first coach was fired shortly after our first game. Players were shuffled between teams like used cars at auction. Two teams went out of business before the end of the first season.

Marketing was an adventure. No successful models existed for selling a women's team sport. No one knew whether they were marketing basketball or women, sport or sex, players or pin-ups. The confusion led to an awkward and unfocused combination of basketball and burlesque. The attractive athletes on the team, whether good players or not, were often asked to pose in provocative clothing and postures that suggested the activity had a hooker quality to it. At the same time, the games more often resembled roller derby than basketball. The skill level across the league was not high and rough play often substituted for basketball proficiency.

Our second coach was a man named Tony. He was a 6'3" shooting guard who had had a successful career playing basketball for the University of Minnesota. He was not of NBA caliber but was good enough that, after college, he had played professionally in Europe for several years.

Tony's coaching experience was limited. He had assisted for a year at Minnesota and acted as a player-coach his last few years in Europe. He certainly knew the game, both technically and tactically. The WBL job was his first stint coaching women. He plunged ahead eagerly, confident that the only differences between male and female professional basketball players were physical size and strength.

Tony was the embodiment of the mantra that "life is a contest." He loved to compete. Each day before practice, he would engage someone in a game of one-on-one or HORSE. In drills, he would substitute for an injured player, always gleefully whipping the player who was guarding him. He took a deck of cards on road trips and was constantly dealing a new hand. An incessant barrage of teasing, taunting, and verbal baiting accompanied all his play. He made all of life into a competitive event.

I had a rocky relationship with him. We shared a love of the game and competitive personalities, but beyond that we agreed on nothing. I was a radical feminist at that time, angry at the world for the way it was and determined to change it. He was a traditionalist. He had lived the charmed life of a star male athlete and thought all was right with the status quo. He thought I was physically talented and fairly smart, but needlessly distracted by femi-nazi mumbo-jumbo. I thought he was hardworking and capable, but the embodiment of a male chauvinist pig.

We frustrated each other immensely. I insisted he use gender-neutral language when instructing us, that he say "player-to-player defense" instead of "man-to-man defense," that he say "block out your player" instead of "block out your man." To his credit, he acquiesced to these requests even though he found them cumbersome and senseless. I always corrected him when he reverted to masculine nomenclature. He hated my nitpicking, especially since the significance of inclusive language was completely lost on him.

Under duress, he often reverted to the language of his past. Our second year, we made the playoffs. Early in our first game, one of my teammates knocked the ball loose. I chased it, but not with the all-out effort he desired. He leaped off the bench and screamed at me from the sideline, "You chased that ball just like a damn woman!"

He was angered by the lack of intensity in my effort, and this was his way of chastising me in the harshest manner possible. His tying my failure to femaleness was ridiculous in this context, but a routine part of the feedback loop in his former life.

His insensitivity to the implications of his remark enraged me. I screamed back at him, "Well, what in the hell do you think I am?" My insubordination earned me a seat on the bench until my rebounding was missed and Tony put me back in the game. We won, and the post-game celebration was full of hugs all around—except between Tony and me. When he approached me with his arms wide, I ducked away and headed for the locker room.

The next day in practice was like any other for Tony. "Hey Kath, you want to play two-on-two against me and Scooter?" He hollered as I entered the gym.

"No," I said sullenly. So he found another player.

The second day after our exchange, he said, "Hey, Kath, want to play HORSE? Bet I kick your butt."

I looked at him with disgust and spit out, "No." He found someone else.

The third day I entered the gym and he came over to me. "Hey, Kath, is something bugging you?"

I struggled to control the fury that was percolating like a volcano inside my stomach. "Is something bugging me?" I said with weakly controlled venom. "Is something bugging me!!" My voice rose in pitch. "Do you know what you said to me in the game the other night?"

In an effort to remember, he furrowed his brow and jutted out his lower lip. Finally, he said, "No, not really. What did I say?"

I told him not only what he had said, but how it had made me feel. Then I told him what it meant, not only for me, but for all the women on our team, in fact for all the women in this fledgling league. How could we succeed when our own coaches equated incompetence with femaleness? Wasn't he supposed to be on our side, promoting the legitimacy of women as athletes?

"This is the whole problem," I said, gathering righteous momentum. "Men like you, who don't even realize they are bigots. This is the reason women have never been given a decent chance in sports, in fact it goes well beyond sports, why women haven't been given a chance in life in general."

At this point in my diatribe, he raised both hands in a symbol of surrender. "I'm sorry," he said, shaking his head from side to side, "I don't remember what I said, and it certainly wasn't meant to hurt your feelings. But, give me a break, Kath, it was in the middle of the game. I just reacted. Do you ever forget anything? You get so caught up in this feminist manifesto BS, you forget we are here to play basketball. Have you ever stopped to think how good you could be if you would let go of all this other stuff? Give it a rest and just play!!"

As time passed, Tony became more introspective about his experience coaching women athletes. One day he said to me after practice, "You focus so much on these male/female things, but you know I don't really even think of you guys as women. I think of you only as basketball players. I could walk into a locker room with all of you naked and not be the least bit aroused."

"Is that so," I sniped. "Then why do you wear cologne to practice every day? I suppose that's a habit you picked up in Europe."

"No, really," he said, ignoring my sarcasm. "How I see you every day—sweaty, hair pulled back, no make-up—it just takes all the sexual attraction out of it." By his talk, our athleticism had neutered us for him. His behavior, however, did not support his assertion. Beside the cologne, he flirted incessantly with several of the women on the team and was always making sexually-laden remarks around us.

I chalked up his comment to his hidebound assumptions about gender, and his behavior to ignorance and habit. I wanted to be treated like and respected as an athlete, but I did not care for his insinuation that women athletes must trade athleticism for sex appeal.

During another moment of self-reflection, he said to me, "You know, Kath, I could never date you. I wouldn't know how to act. When I was dating my wife, I would call her up and say, 'Let's go out Saturday night. I'll pick you up at seven o'clock, we'll go to a movie, and then we'll go to Dillons for dinner.' And, that's what we did. If I was dating you, I'd feel like I'd have to say, 'What time do you want to go? Is a movie OK? What do you want to see?'"

"What's wrong with that?" I shot back. "Heaven forbid that you have to share decision-making and you can't just tell someone what to do."

"It's all part of setting an agenda for who does what," he answered. "When I was dating my wife, I knew what I was supposed to do, she knew what she was supposed to do, all the way to sleeping together if we got that far. With you, by the time we got to sex, I'm sure I'd be impotent. I wouldn't have a clue as to my role—do I initiate? do you?—I'd be so stressed, I'd be worthless."

The blunt honesty of his comment is what made me remember it. Tony viewed himself as "a ladies' man" and for him to admit that there was a circumstance that would intimidate him, much less something as simple as negotiating the starting time of a date or the choice of a movie, indicated the fragile underpinnings of his outward cockiness.

I was too busy battling Tony to realize what he was teaching me. The man I married six years later was considerably more progressive than Tony. He too had been a star athlete in high school and college, but neither his personal identity nor his sexual identity was tied to traditional male roles. Yet our frequent reversal of conventional roles regarding work, career, and home life often caused tension in our relationship.

Several months after I had received a promotion and significant pay raise, my husband said to me, "I feel as if you don't need me anymore." Reacting defensively, I said, "I may be doing better than when we married, but I did not marry you because I *needed* you. I thought it was a choice based on companionship and compatibility then and I'm hoping it still is today."

After further discussion, I realized that his lament was his way of expressing the uncertainty that Tony had voiced years earlier. He was questioning his value to our relationship. My high profile job and larger salary, historically symbols of male success, made him feel anxious. His training in the male world gave him a zero sum perspective—my gains were his losses. My success, which he intellectually applauded and avidly supported, still caused him considerable personal anxiety.

Keeping Score

For men, the score is the measurement of the success or failure of the exercise, task, or activity. Their attitude is, "If you don't keep score, why play?" The thrill of competition is tied to measurement and comparison.

For women, sport is a social activity as much as a competitive one. Whether a game of golf, tennis, or volleyball, the group involved and the interrelationships of the participants are just as important as the activity. The game is the reason for the gathering, but the gathering is as important as the game.

My boss's wife plays tennis with a group of women every Tuesday morning. At lunch one day, she mentioned that she was particularly worn out from that morning's game.

I asked her, "Did you win?" She said she had no idea because they never kept a score. I asked why not. She explained that the point of the activity was to improve their individual games, get a physical workout, and spend pleasant time with friends. The judgmental nature of scorekeeping was counterproductive to these goals.

The very reason that scorekeeping is so important to men makes it disruptive to women. For men, the score tells them where they stand in relation to others playing the game, whether they are ahead or behind in the pecking order. They are more comfortable with this knowledge than without it.

The opposite is true for women. Scorekeeping segregates people into winners and losers, thus disrupting the connections of their network. This segregation produces anxiety.

The Score Card

In my fundraising role, I play a fair amount of golf with donors and supporters. Depending on the gender of my playing partners, the routine at the course is markedly different.

When I play as the only woman in a foursome, we play by *men's rules*. We arrive at the course an hour ahead of our tee time, run into the grill for a hot dog, bag of chips, and a coke, wolf down our food, and head to the practice area to hit balls. We arrive at the first tee about 10 minutes before our tee time and begin negotiating bets and talking about our games.

When men play golf, scorekeeping is an elaborate ritual. Frequently there are multiple games going on within the larger game. We may play "pass the trash," with low net, and a skins game all at the same time. Score reporting, scorekeeping, and cumulative bet tallying are as much a part of the activity as the golf itself. Most of the conversation is good-natured insults about who is sandbagging, who is carrying whom, and bantering about golf—the who, what, where, and how of the game, equipment, and courses.

When I play in a foursome of women, we play by *women's rules*. We plan to meet an hour before our tee time to eat lunch in the clubhouse. We are always running a little late, but usually decide to eat inside anyway. We order turkey sandwiches on wheat bread—hold the mayonnaise because we are all on diets—drink water with lemon and get so involved in conversation that we usually do not have time to hit any balls. No problem, we think, we'll just warm up on the course.

After a stop in the bathroom, we arrive at the first tee about two minutes late for our tee time. Before we hit, we have a discussion about whether we want to keep score that day or not. The decision is a personal one—if someone is playing poorly and opts out of scorekeeping, that is fine with the rest of us. If all of us decide to keep our scores, the next debate is who will record it, because no one relishes this burdensome task.

Frequently, during the play, we get lost in conversations about everything but golf. We may even forget to post a hole or two. The re-creation of our scores can become comical, as we will refuse to give each other anything higher than a triple bogie on the scorecard. Instead of being an intimate part of the activity, scorekeeping is totally peripheral to the social interaction.

I experienced another version of scorekeeping when I played professional basketball. Since the Women's Basketball League was new, we spent a fair amount of time engaged in promotional activities. We held free throw shooting contests in malls; we appeared on local radio and television programs; we handed out dollar-off admissions coupons at grocery stores.

The toughest part of these appearances was the constant challenges from men. Guys in my apartment complex wanted to play one-on-one; overweight business men in suits and wingtips dared us to take on their lunch league; waiters wanted to arm wrestle; and bell boys wanted to race. These men marked their lives on a scorecard. Challenging us to combat, even though only verbally, was part of the game they were living. They wanted to compete and measure themselves against us.

At the time, I thought they challenged us because we were women engaged in a traditionally male activity. Although I still think that turf protection was one of the reasons for these challenges, I have come to realize that this repartee is a routine part of male interchange.

I found their banter threatening and fatiguing. I felt on guard and edgy in my interactions with males. For the men, this gauntlet was part of everyday life. Proving oneself is what they did for a living. For me, the challenges were wearisome and segregating.

Women communicated differently with us. They never asked us to compete. They either viewed us as pioneers or anomalies. Some expressed enthusiasm for what we were doing and lamented that they never had opportunities for athletic activities. Many told us proudly about their children's athletic exploits. Still others viewed us with curiosity or ignored our attempts to stimulate their interest. None challenged us to a footrace or a friendly game of one-on-one.

Dealing with Failure

As much as our worldviews affect the way we evaluate winning, they also influence our attitudes toward losing. The coping mechanisms we adopt for dealing with failure are unique to each gender, reflecting different systems of rewards and penalties and different fears and values.

The continuously competitive nature of the male culture means that losing is, to some extent, inevitable. In all contests, half the participants lose. Boys growing up in this culture have two options—learn how to deal with losing or don't play. Because, for most boys, competitive play is fun and winning an incredibly addictive elixir, many come back to the game time after time seeking that high.

The non-competitive incubator of the female web does not teach women how to deal with losing. Among most girls, cooperative, non-competitive play is the norm and is defined as fun. The judgmental outcomes of winning and losing are antithetical to the closeness that females value, and are therefore avoided in play activities. The consequence is that girls get little practice handling failure.

Athletic Potential

Several years after our marriage, my husband, Mark, and I were on a long drive from Kentucky to Michigan. We had not yet found books on tape and, even though we had dated for years before our marriage, now and then we still discovered new things about each other.

We had both been collegiate athletes of note. We were each well aware of the other's accomplishments, but had rarely discussed what we considered to be our failings as athletes.

He had been an All-American in college, excelling as a quarter-miler and long-jumper on the track team. To this day, a life-sized photograph of him hangs in the entryway to the campus gymnasium. After college and a tour of duty in Vietnam, he had competed at an elite level on the Marine Corps track team.

I had played on two nationally competitive college volleyball and basketball teams. My senior year, I had been a nominee for the Wade Trophy, the highest honor given to female collegiate basketball players. My junior year, I had been a member of the Junior National Volleyball Team. After college, I had played two years of professional basketball.

With the advantage of hindsight, we began to discuss whether we had reached our full potential as athletes and if not, why not.

Mark told me his story: He was recruited after high school to play football at Kansas, but opted instead to stay close to home and accept a track scholarship at Central Missouri State. He described his high school coach as a wonderful man who coached every sport, but had no knowledge of weight training and little sophistication in his approach to conditioning. He talked about his high school, a small school with less than one hundred male students. They had meager resources for athletics and competed against schools with much larger enrollments and better facilities. Given better coaching and a better training environment in high school, he figured he could have reached his physical potential. His failure was circumstantial. He could have succeeded in football at Kansas if external conditions had been different, and if he had been better trained.

I told him my story: I was one of very few girls with opportunities to participate in sports as early as junior high and high school because I attended a parochial school. I said my high school coach was also a special person who had taught me much about life. She was not overly knowledgeable as a coach; however, I cited my perfectionist tendencies as a much greater liability to my progress than her lack of technical expertise. I set impossible standards for myself and then punished myself mercilessly when I didn't achieve them; yet, I was so sensitive to criticism that I was almost impossible to coach.

I also talked of my difficulties with authority. After high school, I had been coached by one of the best technicians in the country. Instead of appreciating his expertise and learning from his feedback, I was distracted by his delivery, which I found belittling and abusive. I resisted his instructions, obsessed about our off-court exchanges, and fought him on everything until finally, in total frustration, he dismissed me from his team. I returned home a failure, my pride wounded and my spirit broken. I recovered enough to finish my college career on a successful note, but my dreams of Olympic participation were gone. As recalcitrant as I had been during the experience, I internalized that failure. By my telling, not reaching my potential was my own fault.

Not until later did I realize how our analysis of our experiences typified male and female explanations for failure. My husband placed responsibility outside himself; I placed responsibility inside myself. He blamed his failure on circumstances outside his control, i.e., a lack of coaching expertise and facilities. I blamed my failure on internal shortcomings, i.e. perfectionism and difficulty with authority.

I am sure the truth for both of us lay somewhere in the middle. My husband now admits that he was afraid to go away to school, and that he reveled in being "the big fish in a small pond." I now realize that failure to flourish in an abusive environment is not a character flaw.

However, that day in our storytelling, my husband preserved his image of himself as a good athlete who could have been great given better training conditions; I preserved my image of myself as a good athlete who could have been great had I not been an uncoachable head case.

Externalizing failure preserves self-esteem—*"it wasn't my fault; there was nothing I could do."* Blame is shifted from the self to outside circumstances. When that blame indicts other people, however, females often flinch. My husband revered his high school coach, yet he did not hesitate to blame his failures on the man's lack of expertise. I, too, venerated my high school coach, yet my instinct was to defend her weaknesses. Blame for my shortcomings, therefore, rested solely with me.

The primacy of relationships in the female psyche prioritizes protecting others even if the result is damage to self. Females will at times internalize other's failures as well as their own. Males rarely struggle with this level of codependency.

Fourteen and a Failure

When I was 14 and in the ninth grade, our school decided to move the basketball game with our archrival to the high school gym and schedule it on a Friday night so more people could attend. We would play a doubleheader, with the girls tipping off at 6:30 p.m. and the boys at 8:00 p.m. Our girls' team was good and heavily favored; our boys' team was mediocre and a decided underdog.

On the appointed night, our coach met us in the locker room before the game and told us that since this was a game attended by many parents and family members, she and the opposing team's coach had discussed an arrangement where everyone would get a chance to play. In the third quarter, each coach would play only her second string. Our female mindset of inclusiveness told us all that this was a great idea.

At halftime, we were ahead by five points, a comfortable margin for a junior high girls' game. By the end of the third quarter, we were five points behind, a surmountable margin given the skill of our team. The fourth quarter was a disaster for us. We could not close the five-point gap, and as time grew shorter and the prospect of an upset loomed larger, we made more and more unforced errors, finally losing the game.

The loss hurt me. I was very competitive and a very poor loser. I also felt I should have pulled our team through. I had choked and I knew it. We shared the locker room with the jubilant winning team, but I found a corner away from everyone else where I hid my head in my arms and bawled.

Our coach, whom I adored, found me and asked me to gather my teammates so she could talk to us. She was a college senior who had taken on the coaching duties of the girls' teams as a voluntary "labor of love." She believed in the positive value of athletics, and she really cared about us. She also knew how badly we had wanted to showcase our skills in front of a crowd that included not only our families but also the families of the boys' team. However, when she approached me, I wanted no part of togetherness. From my self-centered closet, I demanded, "Are you going to yell at us?" Tears filled her eyes and she walked away.

I hated myself. As the leading scorer on our team, I had failed to help us win the most important game of the year, and then as captain, my thoughtless rebuke had hurt the person I wanted most to impress. I had failed as a competitor and as a person.

For weeks, people in our school community debated the wisdom of the third-quarter decision. Many argued that our opponent's veteran coach, knowing she had better substitutes, had cunningly outmaneuvered our novice coach. Others argued that the idea, while magnanimous, had cost us the game due to the poor play of our substitutes.

I staunchly defended both our coach's decision and the performance of my weaker teammates, insisting that the loss was my fault and mine alone. I wallowed in self-flagellation, refusing to share the blame even with the other starters. My self-righteous martyrdom was certainly excessive, but it also meshed perfectly with my worldview. I nurturingly protected the people I cared about by hoarding our collective failure as my own.

The tendency to take sole responsibility for failure or at least to claim more than my share stayed with me as I moved from athlete to coach. One of my players told me once, "Just come into the locker room after a loss and scream at us, will you? Anything is better than that martyr stuff. It's not all your fault, you didn't even play. That makes us all feel so guilty."

Believe me, there were enough times when I did my share of hollering, but her remark made me realize that sharing responsibility for failure with my team was a powerful way to encourage accountability in my female athletes. I doubt that a male team would respond the same way. They may be more apt to let someone else take the blame for failure. In fact, they would be so flabbergasted that someone would actually volunteer, particularly an authority figure, that they would readily allow all responsibility to shift to the willing victim. Women, on the other hand, seem to share a penchant for joining the groveler.

The most dramatic and obvious impact of this difference in dealing with failure may be in our gender-related affinities for competition. In the "life is a contest" world of maleness, objectifying failure helps maintain enthusiasm for "fighting another day." In the "life is a family reunion" world of femaleness, personalizing failure adds significant risks to "fighting another day."

The Results of Competitive Achievement

For males, the benefits of winning, especially in sporting events, are very obvious. The hierarchical structure plainly rewards the male in the one-up position. He has higher status, he owns the bragging rights, and he controls the agenda. In many ways, he is more "manly" than the male in the one-down position.

This direct correlation between worldview and winning is absent for females. They also experience the rewards of competitive achievement—status, bragging rights, and agenda control. The difference lies in the value of these rewards in terms of self-esteem and relationships with others. The female goal of being at the center of connections is not necessarily enhanced by winning. Women who win may, in certain contexts, actually lose.

When recruiting elite high school volleyball players to play on my women's college team, I regularly encountered athletes who were ostracized because of their competitive achievement. The parents of the athletes were often dismayed at the vindictiveness directed toward their daughters by teammates and other parents.

The young women themselves eagerly anticipated college volleyball where, they perceived, all the players would be highly skilled. They thought in college their drive and athleticism would not mark them as different. They wanted success, had spent hours honing their skills and earning their accolades, yet they craved a place where they "fit in."

Winning may also negatively affect relationships with men. In activities that our society associates with masculinity, women who win may be viewed as unfeminine.

Matina Hoerner, in her work on achievement motivations, said,

> "Women appeared to have a problem with competitive achievement, and that problem seemed to emanate from a perceived conflict between femininity and success, … when success is likely or possible, threatened by negative consequences they expect to follow success, young women become anxious and their positive achievement strivings become thwarted. … [T]his fear exists because for most women, the anticipation of success in competitive achievement activity, especially against men, produces anticipation of certain negative consequences, for example, threat of social rejection and loss of femininity." (4)

Who Is Ever Going to Marry You?

I was in my mid-twenties, single, and coaching volleyball at a Midwestern university when I was asked to substitute for a sick wife in a mixed doubles tennis outing. The event was as much social as competitive. The hours of tennis were matched with equal hours of eating and drinking. Men and women were paired at random, the only stipulation being that spouses could not play together. I drew Jack, a college administrator in his early fifties, who had average tennis skills but above-average competitive drive.

Jack held his racquet like a large frying pan and had a penchant for drifting into the middle of the court when he played at the net. He was a big fellow and could swat down all but well-placed shots. I was young and agile and could run from side to side behind him and return the shots that got by him. We made a good team, defeating all of our opponents.

Jack was especially thrilled when we defeated the athletics director, a man who prided himself on his tennis ability, and who was just as competitive as Jack. In fact, when I aced the athletics director to win the set, Jack could barely contain his glee. He threw his racket in the air and gave me a bear hug, all the while effusively praising my game. "That was so good!" he gushed. "You are incredible! Aced him, bam! He never moved. Wow, what a serve!" Then, suddenly, he released me from his hug, gripped my shoulders in both his hands and, holding me at arm's length said, "Oh my God, who is ever going to marry you?"

The not-so-hidden message in his comment was that, in his mind, I made a great mixed doubles partner, but my athletic prowess made me a lousy marriage prospect. The greater my success as an athlete, the more suitors I eliminated. From Jack's perspective, no man would marry a woman knowing he was one-down as an athlete.

The link between gender and athletic prowess is exactly the opposite for males. When a male succeeds athletically, he is rewarded with high reinforcement of his gender identity. He is regarded as the prototype of his sex—the alpha male. Other males seek his company and friendship, and he is perceived as having his choice of female companions. These social rewards motivate men to achieve. Winning is linked to manliness.

Failure carries an equally powerful set of penalties for males. Losing makes them feel "less manly"—it is associated with gender diminishment. In 1994, our University of Kentucky football team played at the University of Florida. We lost 73-7. Describing the effect that loss had on our team, one of our coaches said the players felt like a woman who had been raped. He said the margin of defeat not only embarrassed them, but also made them feel shamed and powerless.

The association of competitive failure with femininity is a prevalent and powerful motivational prod for males. To fail is to fail in "being a man."

For females, losing is mitigated by the socialized assumption that "getting along" is preferable to conflict. This attitude differs markedly from the male assumption that "whatever it takes" is preferable to failure.

I was visiting a volleyball player who had competed for my alma mater several years after I graduated. They had experienced one of the worst years in the history of the program. With their 5-25 record, they had finished last in the league. My friend told me that, from her perspective, the year had been a great success. The team had really bonded through the adversity of losing. Their support network had actually been strengthened by their collective failure. She said it was one of the most tightly knit teams she had ever been part of and that closeness, for her, made the losing less painful.

Females face a veritable kaleidoscope of possible responses to winning and losing. Besides the rewards that accompany winning, they may face ostracism from peers and questioned gender identity. Besides the penalties that accompany losing, they may experience the positive outcomes of emotional closeness and strengthened relationships. This kaleidoscope produces a wide spectrum of incentives and disincentives for achievement. As opposed to the clarity of the male situation, the consequences of competitive achievement are ambiguous for women.

The Nature of Contests

Males define contests as self-contained events during which normal rules of decorum may be momentarily suspended. Females define contests as just another activity and expect all the usual rules of decorum.

This male ability to separate life into interactions that count and those that don't is ideally suited to their "life is a contest" mentality. Contests have a defined beginning and ending and, within them, males tolerate what would otherwise be aberrant behavior. Since winning is the shared goal of the males competing in the contest, this "whatever it takes" attitude is accepted as a necessity, and is often glorified, idealized, and mimicked.

Females do not easily compartmentalize life into contests and "the rest." For women, relationships are ongoing and primary. Relationship standards supersede contest standards, meaning *everything counts*. The stresses associated with competing are no excuses for abandoning civil behavior.

Temper Tantrums

I recall playing for a male coach who had a quick temper. When we played poorly, he became very abusive, calling us names, throwing things around the locker room, and screaming strings of personalized obscenities. These tirades had an effect on the team that lasted several days. We withdrew from him, often becoming sullen and recalcitrant. We refused to interact with him in any playful or casual manner. Our behavior puzzled him immensely. He saw no correlation between his behavior in the locker room and the following day.

In his mind, his locker room behavior was a predictable reaction to our poor performance. It showed that he cared deeply about winning and was not going to take losing lightly. After the loss was behind us, he thought we should re-group as a team and collectively prepare for the next contest. Clinging to past failures or exchanges now became self-destructive behavior.

For us, the post-match tirades were personal attacks. We internalized his hurtful words, and their pointlessness only intensified the damage. We were incapable of dismissing his remarks as harmless temper tantrums that allowed him to blow off steam. They counted, and the next day they continued to be part of our relationship with each other. To us, no loss was devastating enough for that level of personal malevolence.

Memories of those destructive tirades had an effect on me when I entered the coaching ranks myself. I knew my competitive nature predisposed me to this type of behavior. I hated losing, and the helplessness I felt as a coaching spectator on the sideline triggered intense frustration and rage. I was so afraid of repeating those ruinous spectacles that I did not enter a locker room after a contest for the first six years of my coaching career.

At first, I considered going to the locker room only after we had won. However, I realized that my female athletes would interpret that behavior as a message that I cared about them only if we succeeded. I knew that conditioning my affection on the outcome of a contest would seriously weaken my relationship with them. Consequently, I denied my team and myself the shared joys of victories to avoid the pain I was likely to inflict after losses.

The safeguards I took with post-match locker rooms, however, did not save me from inflicting damage during contests. I remember more than one occasion in which I hurt a player's feelings with the content, intensity, or tone of my criticism during a match. With few exceptions, winning the competition did not nullify that hurt for my female athletes.

I recall one particularly important match for my volleyball team. With a win, we would move into the top 10 in the national rankings. We all felt the stress created by the opportunity. Neither coaches nor athletes performed particularly well during the match, but despite our anxiety, we had a chance to win.

During a tense part of the match, I shouted harshly at one of my star players. After winning a close fifth game, she refused to join in the post-match hugs and celebration. When I approached her, she snarled at me, "I don't even care that we won; I can't stand you!" My rebuke had hurt her. Even though she was intensely competitive, in her mind, my behavior was not excusable in the interests of winning. I learned that day that the contest was an ongoing part of our relationship, not exempt from it.

My experience as an athlete and a coach is that females *never forget*. The importance of relationships to our self-esteem may, at times, affect our desire to compete. Victory and defeat both lose significance in the face of conflict.

Forgotten a Moment Later or Remembered Forever

I was sitting at the scorer's table watching the annual Indiana versus Kentucky men's basketball game in 1998. Freedom Hall was sold out to one-half Indiana fans and one-half Kentucky fans. A national television audience was watching and the clock was running out on an Indiana comeback.

One of the younger Indiana players committed a lazy reaching foul that put Kentucky at the free throw line. The Indiana team captain grabbed the younger player by the arm and violently turned him around. "No fouls!" he screamed into his face, still gripping his arm. The younger player screamed back, "I didn't f—king touch him," and roughly jerked his arm free. Unrelenting, the captain got so close to the younger player that their chests were touching and said through clenched teeth, "Settle down, damn it! I said, 'No fouls.'" Seething, the younger player turned away and took his position in the backcourt.

Several seconds later, the younger player hit a three-point shot at the buzzer that tied the game and sent it into overtime. Bedlam broke loose on the Indiana side of the gym. The young player turned and leaped into the outstretched arms of the team captain, wrapping his legs around his waist. The captain carried the exuberant goat-turned-star to the Indiana bench, where he was mobbed by the rest of the team. Their angry exchange was vaporized instantaneously in that moment of exaltation.

When I was a senior in college, our Michigan State volleyball team traveled to the West Coast to compete in a tournament at UCLA. We were the best team in our region of the country, but California volleyball presented us with a whole new set of challenges.

One of our matches was against the team from Pepperdine University. They were not a powerful team per se, but a crafty group that understood the game better than we did. We were taller and more athletic and did not think we should be losing, but we were.

On one play, their setter fooled me completely with the direction of her set. I did not get to my block on the sideline in time, leaving the hitter with a wide-open shot. Cate, one of my teammates and my best friend, charged into the middle of the court from her position on the baseline. The Pepperdine player hit the ball over Cate's head, right into the place she had vacated.

I turned around and yelled angrily, "Geez, Cate, she's a deep-court hitter!"

I don't remember if we won or lost that match. After all, it happened way back in 1976. I do clearly remember that Cate did not speak to me for three days. And, although we can laugh about it now, I know her recollection of that hurtful rebuke is as vivid as mine.

Fair Play

Another tangent of our attitudinal differences shows up in the debate as to what constitutes "fair play." "Whatever it takes" as a *modus operandi* is distinct from "let the best player win." Each defines a different set of boundaries for task accomplishment. Given that both approaches are "within the rules," neither is inherently more noble or just than the other, but each feels more comfortable to one gender than to the other.

Racquetball

I used to play racquetball with a male friend whom I dated in college. I was a better player than he, having spent more of my childhood playing racquet sports. He was, however, strong and fit, and also competitive, so I never beat him without a battle.

He had one very irritating habit: when he hit a bad shot that set me up for an easy kill, he would crowd the area of my next swing, leaving me with no options other than to hit him with the ball or my racquet, or call "a hinder," the racquetball equivalent of a foul. A hinder call stopped play, and the point was replayed from the beginning.

Initially, I simply called a hinder and we replayed the point. Soon, however, I realized that his interference was intentional. This angered me. A few times, I pasted him in the backside when he blocked my swing. He winced, but always returned to the service area grinning, clearly pleased with his tactic for gaining a replay. This fueled my agitation. It also dampened my competitive spirit. More than once, I left the court vowing never to play him again.

I felt that his way of competing was unfair. I thought it bordered on cheating—he had made a mistake and, instead of suffering the consequences, he was forcing me to choose between hitting him or stopping play—each of which resulted in the replaying of the point.

One day, I pointed out to him that his way of competing was not pitting my skills against his in a straightforward fashion. It was not playing *by the spirit of the rules*.

He disagreed, saying his practice was perfectly legal and telling me that he had learned it playing handball with his father, an ordained minister. He said fairness had nothing to do with it; we were engaged in a competition, and were both allowed to take whatever advantages we could get within the rules. Further, he contended that if his habit upset me and adversely affected my game, then he had earned yet another perfectly legitimate edge. He claimed his tactics were well *within the confines of the rules*, and therefore totally fair.

At times like these, I thought this guy was a total jerk. Now I'm married to him, quite happily most of the time. We still routinely debate issues of fairness and we are only slightly closer to agreement than we were in college.

Mariah Burton Nelson says in her book *Embracing Victory*, "… cheating is cheating only if both participants have agreed to the rules beforehand." (5) My future husband and I had not. He was playing by male rules—"whatever it takes"; I was playing by female rules—"may the best player win."

In *Hardball for Women*, Pat Heim explains these differences in viewpoint: "Men like to win; women like to be fair. While boys are told 'it doesn't matter whether you win or lose, it's how you play the game,' very few ever believe it. If you're going to play a game, the point is to win. For girls, on the other hand, relationships are what matter. Being fair enhances closeness and equality." (6)

My male opponent was competing *within the rules*. I was competing *by the rules*. Each of us defined our method as *fair*.

These "by the rules/within the rules" distinctions are, however, neither dichotomous nor immutable. My own attitudes about fair play shifted over time from an innocent "by the rules" definition to a more pragmatic "within the rules" definition.

The change coincided with my transition from player to coach, from the world of play to the world of work, from the realm of inconsequence to the realm of consequence. These changes redefined the importance of winning, giving me an insider's look at the male dilemma. Suddenly, the game was more than "only a game;" it was my job, my reputation, and my career.

In volleyball, when a hitter attacks the ball, the opposing team tries to block it. If the ball goes out of bounds, it may be debated who touched the ball last: the hitter or the blocker on the opposing team. The officials are charged with evaluating the play and rendering an immediate judgment as to who caused the wayward shot. Their ruling obviously favors one team and penalizes the other.

The blocker knows whether she touched the ball, regardless of whether the official saw it. The lead official may ask for help on "touch" calls from the other official or the line judges. The fairness question is—if the official misses the call, should the blocker volunteer "a touch"?

While competing in college, an opposing coach commended me on my sportsmanship for admitting "a touch" on a missed call. As a coach, I encouraged my team to do the opposite. I told them that the officials were paid to make those calls. If they missed a touch and it resulted in our advantage, it was a legitimate edge that would be balanced by missed calls that worked to our disadvantage.

Hindsight makes my early reactions seem naive and idealistic, although also nostalgically wholesome and honest. Admitting to "a touch" was certainly the more just way to compete. The opposing player had made a good play by hitting the ball off my hands out of bounds. I knew it; the fact that the officials missed the call was irrelevant. My admission was a "by the rules" interpretation of fair play.

Leaving the call to the judgment of the officials was a more pragmatic way to compete. It depersonalized the contest by adding a third-party arbitrator and removing the honor system from our exchanges. My teams' illegitimate gains were "bad calls" and therefore "within the rules" of fair play.

It would be both spurious and strident to link these two attitudes specifically with gender. Males are fully capable of honest, letter-and-spirit-of-the-rule competition, and females are fully capable of barracuda-like, win-at-all-costs fervor. However, a generalized gender linkage is appropriate due to the relative importance of winning in our respective lives.

The challenge for males is to combat the incessant message of the hierarchical world that winning is everything, and therefore any edge is a legitimate edge. The challenge for females is to recognize the debilitating message that winning is tainted, and honorable losing always more virtuous. Pragmatic righteousness is somewhere in the middle.

Responses to Authority

Pat Heim talks of the different ways males and females view authority. She says:

"… Men and women have learned different guidelines about authority … . From childhood on, most men become accustomed to living their lives in … hierarchical organizations … . The leader expects that when he gives an order, it will be followed. Without this chain of command, he believes all will be chaos … . [Women perceive organizations] as a flat playing field where everyone is equal, and when it comes to solving problems and mapping out the next play, flatness implies collaboration and equality." (7)

Exactly What Privileges Does Rank Have?

I remember participating in a volleyball practice when one of my teammates became frustrated and cursed loudly. Our male coach became furious. He called us together and ordered us to stand in a line in front of him. He began his tirade by saying, "I get so damn mad when you girls swear!" The irony of his remark tickled me and, although I knew he was angry, I involuntarily laughed out loud. Using several more expletives, he ordered me to "start running." I finished the practice circling the gym as punishment for my defiance.

Later, we had a heated debate about his reaction to the swearing player. He saw nothing incongruous about his expletive-filled retort—a fact I found unbelievable. He argued that he was the head coach and that it was his right to set the rules for behavior in the gym. He had grown up at a time when "ladies" did not swear and he argued that his position allowed him to impose on us his standards for our behavior. We had no reason to expect that these standards would apply to him.

I thought his position was patently unfair. I had no trouble with the coach setting behavioral standards in the gym; in fact, I agreed that was his right. However, I balked at his contention that the standards were rightfully unilateral. According to my bias, rank had privileges limited by fairness, not power.

Later, when I was coaching my own women's team, I gained an appreciation for his perspective. I benched one of my players for an emotional outburst directed at an official, and then tried to defend myself when I angrily and loudly objected to a call. She questioned, just as I had, why I should be allowed behavior that she was not. I argued that my rank as head coach entitled me to certain latitude, that my impact with the officials would be more significant than hers, and that my outbursts were probably less emotional and, therefore, more pointed, than hers.

Her reaction to my arguments was the same as mine had been years earlier. In her mind, my discipline was unfair. She did not see the world in terms of hierarchical levels, each imbued with certain unquestionable rights. She was willing to accept my instruction and guidance, but she saw no justification for different behavioral standards. My authority was confined to limits I too was willing to accept.

I learned from the women I coached that their view of authority was the same as the one I had held as an athlete. Whenever I tried a "my way or the highway" approach, they subtly reminded me of our commonality. They would do anything I ordered if they understood it and were convinced it was the optimal way to proceed. If not, they would question me, fight me, and even sabotage me if I did not bend.

My athletes wanted direction, they wanted leadership, but they also wanted to have input. They knew I was the boss, but they expected me to value their opinions, to listen to them even if I disagreed, and to welcome their feedback. They did not consider it disrespectful to question my decisions. In fact, they viewed it as their responsibility. After all, they reasoned, they were just trying to improve our shared situation.

Through trial and error, I was learning another truism: *women do not let other women act like men*. Even if a woman is clearly in a leadership role, as I was as the head coach, my female underlings had different expectations of me than they would have had of a male in the same position. They expected more understanding and compassion, they demanded more say, and they tolerated less abuse.

In disciplining my teams, I strayed outside acceptable boundaries numerous times during my coaching career. Usually, I was yanked rudely back into reality.

Settle Down!

One of my early teams was above average and led by a stalwart middle blocker named Leigh. We were preparing for an important conference match and, in my game plan, I had made repeated reference to a fake play that our opponent loved to run. I cautioned my team, especially my middle blockers, to make sure they watched for some obvious cues that the fake was coming and held their position on the floor. The fake was a key part of our opponent's offense, and I was adamant that we stop it early. I reviewed this key with my team repeatedly.

With us leading 5-3 in the first game, they did exactly what I had predicted. Their best player jumped into the air near the net and dropped her hands to chest level—the two clues I had given my team. Then, she set a quick ball to their middle blocker. Leigh, my veteran captain, fell for the fake—she jumped with the first player, leaving her teammate open for an uncontested crushing spike.

The gym erupted in pandemonium. The opposing team went crazy. Their bench leaped to their feet and high-fived each other; all ten spectators cheered wildly.

I also went crazy. I jumped out of my seat, screaming, "Leigh, it's the fake! What are you thinking! You didn't even listen." Leigh knew before my outburst that she had made a mistake. She winced, shaking her head up and down, and pointing at herself as she listened to my tantrum.

I continued berating her. "I can't believe it! You, of all people! You didn't even listen! Who am I supposed to count on?" My voice rose higher in pitch. "Where is your head, anyway? You're not even paying attention!" Finally, she said in exasperation, "Judas Priest, Kathy, will you settle down!"

The official, having heard the entire exchange in the almost-empty gym, slapped Leigh with a penalty for swearing at me and told me to sit down. I benched Leigh immediately and, fuming, took my seat.

The opposing team seemed to gain momentum from the chaos on our side of the net. They scored six straight points. I knew we could not win the match without Leigh on the court. At 5-10, I put her back in. We won that game and the next two for a decisive 3-0 victory.

Leigh and I never discussed our exchange, but I had obviously stepped outside of acceptable bounds, and I knew it. Leigh was a very coachable athlete; she worked hard, she competed hard. She willingly took direction and played the game with enthusiasm and energy.

But there were limits to what she would tolerate from me. When I exceeded those limits, she corralled me even if the consequence was sitting on the bench. The competition lost significance for her. My rank as a superior did not transcend our connection as women. That bond prescribed certain decorum in my behavior.

Undoubtedly, for women the most baffling aspect of dealing with those in authority is the capricious use of power. We have no reference points for explaining this type of behavior in our gender Rolodex, so we perceive it as totally irrational and needlessly despotic.

Even though males do not like being the object of the whimsical exercise of authority, they understand it better than females do. In a pyramidally-structured world, power is by definition unevenly distributed and, until you have it, indifference is the best tactic for dealing with its abuse.

Pat Heim attempts to explain the phenomenon to women by re-naming the exploitation, "loyalty tests." She says, "Most men in leadership positions constantly assess if those around them recognize their power to lead. To do so, they assert their authority by using loyalty tests. These can take the form of seemingly illogical, oddball requests or circumstances … . By nature, loyalty tests must be outlandish—if they made perfect sense, they wouldn't verify your loyalty." (8)

Loyalty Tests

A coaching friend shared this incident: One of his counterparts had become so enraged by the failure of his women's volleyball team to defeat a particular opponent that he had ordered his team back to the gym at midnight. When they arrived, he had buckets and rags ready. Telling them they were not worthy to play on the court, only to mop it, he made them get on their hands and knees and scrub the playing court. I said, "What a demeaning activity; what was the purpose?" My colleague laughed at the inanity of my question. "Purpose?" he said. "It had no purpose. He was mad."

I asked if the offending coach's team played better after this humiliation. He said they had defeated an inferior opponent the next day, although they were obviously tired. It was early in the season, he explained, and the coach had to send a message as to what was acceptable. The team was accustomed to these antics, he told me, and he thought they would regain their competitive fire.

The incident reminded me of a similar stunt I had pulled early in my coaching career. We played a match against my alma mater, a contest I wanted to win for all the wrong reasons. I equated victory with validation of myself as a coach. I had left my former mentor with little respect for her coaching skills and I thought my strategy for defeating her team was foolproof.

My team played with little enthusiasm, indifferent to the correlation between my ego and the result of the match. They paid scant attention to the strategy I had designed for victory. We never utilized our superior quickness, and lost the match in four games. I sulked through a post-match social at a parent's house. We returned to campus well after midnight.

The next day, my anger was like cellulite, subcutaneous but obvious to all who cared to take notice. My assistant convinced me not to try to conduct a practice. However, given my state of mind, a day off was out of the question. I told her to bring to practice every rake, shovel, and wheelbarrow she could find in her garage. When the team arrived, we loaded them into a van with our yard tools and took them to my house. Piled in the front yard were two truckloads of topsoil that had been delivered the week before. We gave each player a rake or a shovel, and told them to start digging.

My team was not happy with this assignment. They were tired from the late night and saw no value in my "loyalty test." They sullenly went about their tasks, muttering to each other about the pointlessness of the activity and my inability to "get over a simple loss." I assigned the task of loading and hauling the wheelbarrows full of dirt to myself and my assistant.

This simple decision rescued me from a mutiny. As we worked together, my anger faded and my team was struck little by little with the ridiculousness of what we were doing. They began to tease me, threatening to turn me in to the university ombudsman or to call social services and claim child abuse.

The excursion became a chapter in our program's history, the recounting part of each freshman orientation. As with most folklore, the story grew in scope and hilarity with each telling. I realize now that my participation in the castigation of my team made this only a quasi-loyalty test. By sharing the penalty for losing, I had equalized our positions enough that my team was willing to submit to my capricious exercise of power.

I wish I could say each of my "loyalty tests" had had this bonding effect. I went crazy after a loss one year and ordered my team to my office to watch the film at midnight after the game. I stopped the machine at each error and replayed it over and over, verbally berating the offenders each time. One of my younger, more promising, players quit that night, calling my antics ridiculous and unnecessary.

Another time, I was so upset over a loss that I took the van back to the hotel and made my team walk. The walk was not a long one, but the rejection was painful to my players and one of them shared it with her mother. The parent chastised me sternly for abdicating my supervisory responsibilities and threatened to turn me in to the administration if I ever pulled a stunt like that again. I was irritated at my player for tattling to her mother, but I also had a hard time defending my behavior.

Males generally deal with "loyalty tests" better than females. The you-will-do-it-because-I-can-make-you-do-it method of management is not user-friendly for either gender, but males recognize these power plays as a means to assess obedience and measure devotion. They know the exploitation is not personal, but just part of the game of solidifying rank and discerning faithfulness.

Females generally do not see any value in loyalty tests. To us, they seem inane, if not downright abusive. However, learning to recognize and survive these shenanigans for what they are is one of the mental hurdles we must overcome to survive the game.

Being a Team Player

I watched with interest the behavior of Dot Richardson, the star shortstop of the USA's 1996 Olympic softball team. At the time of the games, she was a 34-year-old medical student finishing up her residency.

When interviewed, she refused to focus on herself or her considerable accomplishments, the items the media found intriguing. After games, she always dragged several teammates with her to interviews, when it was obvious only she had been requested. She insisted on introducing them and lauding their accomplishments. She perceived and portrayed herself as "one of the gang," with no larger role than anyone else. Although to those who watched the competition this was not true, Dot shunned the "star" label in the interest of being a *team player*.

Although the Olympic Games were filled with exemplary displays of team play on both the women's and the men's side, I did not see any male athletes struggling this conspicuously with the "star" role. On the male side, both stars and non-stars seemed comfortable with a team tiered by skill level and the subsequent attention given to the "stars." The preoccupation with inclusiveness and the homogenizing of roles was a decidedly female obsession.

Interdependence, a primary tenet of the female worldview, means that women are most comfortable in *team* situations where they have a role somewhat equivalent to others, especially their clique of friends. Friendship is important on female teams and friendship implies a certain degree of equality.

Not only do girls/women shun the "star" role, they also reject the "grunt" role. Most females have trouble finding value in relatively insignificant roles on a team. Just as males are always keeping score, females are always appraising their place in a group. If they judge their role trivial relative to their peers, they are more likely than males to quit the activity.

On female teams, no honor comes with "carrying the shoes" of the "star." On male teams, any affiliation with the "star" is valuable. To function effectively, therefore, male groups tier themselves, female groups flatten themselves.

Pat Heim says, "Men grow up learning to sacrifice self for the good of the team. They understand that being a good team player means carrying out the agenda of those above them in the hierarchy … [that] for the hierarchy to function properly, everyone must be in his or her assigned position." (9)

Heim and other social scientists frequently credit gender-differentiated childhood play experiences as the basis for these different attitudes about team. Boys, they say, grow up playing games on teams; girls grow up playing with one friend at a time.

However, the root of the difference is deeper than that. I grew up playing team sports, as did Dot Richardson, as did most of the women I coached. Yet all these game-playing "tomboys" still struggle with balancing their desire to be a "standout" with not wanting to stand out.

Women's soccer coach Anson Dorrance said in a Sports Illustrated article:

> "Women are more sensitive and more demanding of each other, and that combination is horrible. Men are not sensitive and not

demanding of each other, and that's a wonderful combination for building team chemistry. We can play with guys who are absolute jackasses. We have no standards for their behavior as long as they can play: *Just get me the ball*. But if a girl's a jerk, even though she gets me the ball, there's going to be a huge chemistry issue: *I don't want to play with her*. But she serves you the best ball on the team! *I would much rather play with So-and-so*. But you're terrible together! *I would rather play with her*. Why? *The other girl's a bitch*. … It's unfathomable to me, but for them this is major." (10)

Best Woman for the Job

In my third year of college, I transferred from a small school to a large university to get away from home and to play intercollegiate athletics at a higher level. I was one of several athletes who were new to the volleyball team at the university. The team trained in pre-season camp for three weeks prior to the start of the school year. We lived in a dormitory, ate our meals together in a school cafeteria, and practiced three times a day. Our constant proximity and the rigor of the training experience bonded us as teammates and friends very quickly.

At the end of the pre-season, we were asked by the coach to vote for a captain. I was the best player on the team, an upperclassman, outgoing, and intensely competitive. In my mind, these characteristics not only qualified me for consideration, but also made me the front-runner for the job. Besides, I desperately wanted to be captain. Despite my outward self-confidence, I craved affirmation from my teammates.

Knowing it was unacceptable to vote for myself, I voted for my best friend. So did everyone else. She won by an overwhelming margin. She was a good player with an engaging personality and a Peter Pan nonchalance that was irresistible. Given the tenuous interpersonal fabric of female teams, she was a better choice than I. Her easygoing manner and quiet confidence made for a more effective leadership style than my in-your-face assertiveness.

I knew all that, but I was still bitterly disappointed. At that moment, I longed for a hierarchical system that rewarded productivity rather than the webbed system, of which I was a part, that functioned better when the leader was a consensus builder.

The hierarchical mindset produces leadership that is status-based and power-driven. Under these parameters, I would have been chosen captain. The web mindset produces leadership that is expertise-based and compromise-driven. Given these parameters, my friend was best suited to the job.

The nature of team attachments is obviously different for men and women and that difference affects their way of thinking about team play. For men, being part of a team means you have colleagues who share the same goals and problems. This commonality bonds you together. You may join each other for social occasions, but your conversations are mostly about the activities of the team. If one of you leaves the team for another team, even a rival team, your interactions are simply less frequent. The difference is largely quantitative, not qualitative. Replacing one set of teammates with another is easy and rather routine.

For women, being part of a team means you have friends who share similar interests and concerns. This link makes emotional closeness possible. Your social exchanges are opportunities to get to know each other outside of the activities of the team, and your conversations are only minimally focused on team matters. If one of you leaves the team for another team, it is emotionally difficult and painful. Not only is your interaction less frequent, it is often less intimate. Replacing one set of teammates with another is complicated and distressing.

Pat Heim devotes an entire chapter to the subject "How to Be a Team Player." She makes an insightful observation about "friendship" versus "friendliness" in differentiating gender attitudes toward connections on teams. She says:

> "Women have friendships; men are friendly. The behaviors initially appear to be the same, but the underlying rules differ. For women, a friend is a friend in all situations: in a meeting, at lunch, when the boss is displeased with your performance, and when you have competing needs. But the friendliness that men practice comes and goes as needed. Women grow up with devotion to their best friends. Men switch sides and loyalties as easily as they shed one team jersey and don another." (11)

When I coached volleyball at the University of Kentucky, I had an assistant coach named Mary. We had similar backgrounds and life experiences, and we really enjoyed each other's company. We socialized together often, either alone or with our respective spouses. We shared our pasts, we shared problems beyond our workplace concerns, and we got to know each other's families. Even though I was her boss, we became very close friends.

After five years, the University of Florida hired Mary as their head volleyball coach. Since Florida and Kentucky are in the same league, we were now direct competitors. The first place I felt the impact was in recruiting. Mary and I liked the same attributes in players and had worked in tandem on developing a prospect list. For the first few years, we were often recruiting the same athletes.

This overlap was very hard on our friendship. The openness and confidential sharing that had characterized our relationship was tempered by the paranoia natural to dealing with a rival. As she became more and more successful, defeating my team repeatedly, my anxiety grew. Our conversations moved from the intimate exchanges of "friendship" to the polite pleasantries of "friendliness." Only after I left coaching did we resume our habit of more intimate sharing, but even then, the distance between us precluded the return of our former closeness.

Leadership

The female predilection to prefer working in a group of equals makes leadership development a real challenge. Women's hesitancy to tell others what to do in a direct and unambiguous manner is a distinct disadvantage when immediate decisions are necessary. Also, our tendency to punish our peers when they do act in this manner provides further disincentive for directness.

When the media reviewed the success of the Kentucky 1998 football team, attention was often focused on the leadership abilities of the star quarterback, Tim Couch. One oft-repeated example was the demanding schedule *he* set for off-season workouts. He would post the workout times on the exit door to the team dormitory. Underneath the time and place for the workout was the following order: "If you can't make it, see me. T.C." Supposedly, no one on the team dared miss a workout and face Tim. So, they all came, and the team improved as a result.

I am sure this story, quickly growing into a legend, is not absolutely true. However, I cannot imagine this type of pseudo-coercion working with a women's team, much less being identified as strong leadership. The female definition of "team" as a group of equals with distinct roles means hierarchy within the group is often viewed as suspect, if not downright dangerous.

Jane and Sara

I coached a gifted volleyball player named Jane, who was extremely competitive, a relentless worker, and, by nature, somewhat shy. She was in a leadership position on my team and I was always encouraging her to be more demanding of her teammates. I felt that if she would insist that they compete and work at her level of intensity, our team would be more successful.

In a heated discussion with me, she blurted out, "I can't tell them what to do; if I do, they won't like me." In frustration, I demanded, "Is it more important for us to win or for your teammates to like you?" My question was rhetorical. By her behavior she had already answered it.

Jane considered herself a good team player and was loved by her teammates. She was easy to get along with and never offensive in words or tone. She was skilled in her role as the setter for our team and worked hard at her individual skills. She quietly and efficiently filled her role in the group. She never considered whether aggressive behavior would make our team more successful. She just knew that it would damage her image of herself as a team player, and that fact was important enough to her that she never risked it on my behalf.

Sara, who played on a different team, was just as competitive and driven to succeed as Jane, but was, at times, despised by her teammates. She would tell other players what to do and would chastise them if they made a mistake or did not play with enough effort. She was the star and she knew it. When matches were on the line, she wanted to be the catalyst for victory, and she often was. Her statistics were impressive, and she was acutely aware of them.

Jane and Sara both played on very good teams at different times during my coaching tenure at Kentucky. It is difficult to judge which player had a bigger impact on our success.

Sara pushed her teammates mercilessly. She was demanding, aggressive, and direct. They were afraid of her wrath and, therefore, often responded to her chiding. But the anxiety created by her behavior made our success less enjoyable. The tension on the court did not dissipate when the match concluded. That team had difficulty enjoying each other's company. They had lots of wins, but little joy.

Jane's team was a close-knit group. They lived together and spent a lot of their off-court time together. Their strength, however, was in part dependent on their closeness. As long as they were all getting along, everyone felt a commitment to the group and gave her best effort. However, when that off-court chemistry broke down, Jane's team had trouble competing.

Jane was very sensitive to team interpersonal problems and played the role of group peacemaker. She always played hard, but at times let her decision-making be influenced by group dynamics more than tactical efficacy. If she was having trouble getting along with a particular player, she had trouble setting her. It was difficult for her to separate her emotional attachments from her performance.

Jane and Sara were both All-Americans; they both led their teams to NCAA Tournament appearances. Jane was pleasant, sometimes to a fault; Sara was tough, sometimes to a fault.

As much as I appreciated and learned from these two, I always yearned for their hybrid, that pleasantly tough cookie who was considerate of her teammates, yet willing to drive them to win.

The America's Cup Experiment

In her book *Making Waves*, Anna Seaton Huntington tells the story of the first all-women's team to compete for the America's Cup. The race is the most prestigious large-boat sailing competition in the world. Bill Koch had skippered the team that won the 1992 Cup and conceived the idea of an all-female squad. He was also the organizer and major financial backer of the venture.

He hired several of the male members from his 1992 team to coach the 1996 women's team. He also had his technical experts develop the Mighty Mary, a technologically superior sailing vessel. Despite these efforts, the team did not even qualify for the America's Cup finals, much less win a consecutive victory.

Huntington's book details the specifics of the team selection process, the preparatory training regimen, and the racing tactics. Both she and Koch speculate on why the team failed to qualify for the finals even though they had superior preparation and equipment. Both cite a lack of leadership as the Achilles' heel that derailed their quest for victory.

Koch takes partial responsibility for the failure. He recalls that his 1992 male team was plagued by constant internal power struggles. He said, "I had to teach the men to get along—to get them not to yell and criticize each other. My focus was teaching them to be less aggressive and assertive—to get their egos down below the ego of the boat." (12) Even though his team succeeded in winning the Cup, he determined that he could do better with a group that was more committed to the team concept. Consequently, he prioritized team play—defined as the willingness to suppress personal agendas for the good of the group—as one of the major components for selection to the 1996 squad.

Simultaneously, he switched from a male squad to a female squad. Huntington posits that the gender shift combined with a selection process that weeded out assertive behavior made the leadership void predictable. She said, "We were not conditioned to handle confrontation with our coaches or among ourselves. The premium was on harmony. Tolerating and avoiding disputes and sticky issues was the most acceptable way of handling conflict. When conflict arose, as it inevitably did, ... our team, from top to bottom, was ill-equipped to deal with it overtly." (13)

When asked by Koch for her opinion on the leadership issue, management consultant Anne Jardim of the Simmons Graduate School said, " ... I didn't think a leader would emerge, ... the women would have to be forced to come up with one. Women tend to generate teams of equals. We're not hierarchical—we operate by consensus ... . Men need to establish hierarchies, find leaders. Women don't." (14)

Hierarchical structures are more conducive to the development of leadership than flat structures. The pyramidal shape of the hierarchy implies that there will necessarily be leaders and followers. The geodesic nature of the web suggests no such division of authority. The ideal male team is like a specialized military unit—vertically integrated role players. The ideal female team is more like a group pajama party.

Most comfortable with hierarchy, males share tacit assumptions about the attributes that warrant leadership status. These characteristics include superior skill, prior experience, aggressiveness, and self-assurance under pressure. Those possessing these attributes are either given leadership roles or they seize them.

Females find the task of choosing a leader in and of itself distasteful. If forced to make a decision, they are as likely to value popularity and congeniality as skill and experience. Females rarely find aggressiveness a qualifying trait for group leadership.

The top-down leadership style is most efficient when decisions must be made quickly and/or when only the leader can see or understand the scope of the problem facing the group. The inclusive leadership style is most effective when the quality of the decision is more critical than its timeliness, when the decision-makers have separate and specific areas of knowledge, and when group buy-in is important to implement action.

The effectiveness of each style will depend on the situation. In the America's Cup scenarios, the synergy created by the selfless, co-dependent parameters for membership on the all-female team was one of its greatest assets; yet that same "team of equals" blinked when peremptory decisions were necessary for success. (15)

The power struggles inherent in the male system of leadership development meant the male team trained under the stresses of "intense internal competition" (16), but that troop was hardened to conflict and confrontation by race time.

Motivation

Anson Dorrance, the male coach of the University of North Carolina's women's soccer team, says this about motivation:

> " … with women, your effectiveness is through your ability to relate. They have to feel that you care about them personally or have some kind of connection with them beyond the game … . To be an effective leader of a men's team, you don't need a personal rapport as long as there is respect. That's the extent of the relationship. That's all that's really required. But in a women's team, respect is only part of it, and it is derived from a personal relationship. Women have to have a sense that you care for them above and beyond their [athletic] abilities." (17)

Freed to Compete

Terry coached women's volleyball at the University of Nebraska. His teams were always nationally competitive. They had advanced to the Final Four numerous times, and played in the final match twice. But, Nebraska had never won a national championship.

I worked with Terry for two weeks in the summer of 1989. He had been selected as the head coach for the World University Games Volleyball Team and I was his assistant. We spent hours together debating strategy, tactics, and motivation, and arguing about gender issues.

He was very business-like in his approach to the game. He never showed any outward emotion with his team, neither openly encouraging nor chastising them. His cerebral approach usually had a steadying effect on his players, but when his team needed emotion, he could not give it.

I remember watching him during one of his National Championship finals. His team had defeated UCLA, the number-one-ranked team in the country, in a methodical upset two nights earlier. Now, they were facing a very talented, but lower-ranked, Long Beach State squad for the National Championship.

Long Beach quickly shut down Nebraska's deadliest hitter, a rangy middle blocker who hit mostly slides behind the setter. Further, their quick pace of attack and deceptive setting negated some of Nebraska's height advantage and their superior blocking. Early in the match, Terry's team was in trouble.

I don't know if a tactical change could have spared his team from defeat that night, but as a spectator I was most struck by Terry's demeanor. Very early in the match, he disengaged from his team. Instead of leaning forward in his seat and yelling instructions to his players, he slouched back, hanging his arms over the back of the bench. He laughed and joked with his assistant coach as if he was an uninterested observer judgmentally watching a talented team self-destruct. He was impassive and cavalier while his team foundered in front of him. Nebraska lost 0-3.

Several years later, Terry had one of his best teams. They were ranked number one in the country, had won several tournaments against other nationally ranked opponents, and had breezed though the early rounds of the NCAA Tournament. Heading to the Final Four in Springfield, Massachusetts, they were proven, they were battle-tested, and they were favored.

Nebraska's main challenger for the national title was to have been Stanford, a recurring nemesis. However, Texas defeated a lackluster Stanford team in the opening semifinal. Nebraska had pummeled Texas twice during the regular season. If his team could defeat Michigan State in the semifinals, the stage seemed set for Terry's first title.

Michigan State was the dark horse of the tournament. State had pulled a stunning upset by defeating higher-seeded Hawaii in Honolulu to advance to the Final Four. They were newcomers to the national championship scene, but they were young, talented, and fearless.

State won a close first game in the best three-of-five semifinal. Nebraska won game two. Game three was a war, with countless lead changes, each team struggling with rhythm and tinkering with tactics. It lasted almost an hour before Michigan State prevailed and went ahead 2-1. With their best chance yet to win the title, Nebraska and Terry were suddenly within a single game of going home without the trophy—again.

Terry had been coaching at Nebraska for twenty years. He had been voted Coach of the Year three times; he had won over five hundred matches, yet he had no national championship. He told me later that between games three and four, he really did not know what to say to his team. They were not playing poorly, no obvious tactical adjustments needed to be made, and he always felt they would win. He let them get water and towels while he conferred with his assistants. Walking into the huddle, he was still wordless. When he arrived, they all looked at him expectantly. He was silent for a moment and then said to them, "I just want you to know that I love you."

Terry's statement was so out-of-character that it caught his team totally by surprise. His captain regrouped quickly enough to parrot a popular commercial, "Well, you're not getting my Bud Light." They all laughed raucously.

The horn sounded, calling the players back to the court. Without any new instructions, the Nebraska team began the most important game of Terry's career.

Nebraska won game four, then game five.

In the post-match interviews, the media was intensely interested in what had happened between games three and four. They had seen the boisterous laughter in the huddle—in and of itself an absurdity given the situation. They had also noted that the Nebraska players had returned to the court joyful, relaxed, and apparently carefree.

In reporting the exchange in the huddle, one of the star players said that Terry's declaration had freed them to "just play." His statement had assured them that their relationship with him was safe regardless of the outcome of the match. Further, the moment of hilarity caused a collective catharsis among the team members so they felt connected and empowered.

The next night, Nebraska and Terry won their first National Championship.

Obviously, our gender-related values have an effect on our propensity to process information, especially under duress. Remember the story in this book's prologue about the male and female athletes who responded so differently to the same motivational speech from the head coach? The words that served to motivate the male athlete and his teammates were a hindrance to the female and her teammates.

I gave a speech on the interplay between gender and competition that was transcribed for a coaching magazine. (18) Afterward, I became engaged in an e-mail conversation with a basketball coach named Jim. He was in his first year coaching high school girls after a successful career with boys. His former athletics director had given him a copy of my speech as a going-away present. He had read it and tossed it, thinking his coaching methods were transferable from boys to girls. He e-mailed me out of frustration after what he thought was a routine disciplinary action had turned into a disastrous evening with his girls' team.

After several weeks of online dialog, he said, "I am still searching for the core reason women play sports. Until I can find that, I don't think I can be a highly effective coach."

"Why do men play sports?" I queried.

He answered, "Sports is the quickest area in which men can prove that they are the best, #1, 'I am *king*.'"

To paraphrase Jim, men play sports because they love sports. Men love competing, action, and proving themselves.

"Women play sports," I e-mailed Jim, "because they love play." Women love games, interaction, and expressing themselves.

Properly motivated women are just as competitive as properly motivated men. The difference is in the motivation, not the competitiveness. *We're-all-in-this-together* strategies work better with females. They mesh a team into a network that feels comfortable and safe to females even though it may feel awkward and stifling to males. Knitted into a group, women feel empowered and obligated to each other to perform.

You-da-man strategies work better with males. They stratify a team into a hierarchy that feels comfortable and familiar to males even though it may feel awkward and isolating to females. Tiered into a chain of command, men feel confident and obligated, each to his specific task.

The motivational approach is different; the competitive result is the same.

Specific words are not the only hazard for coaches of women—tone can also be a pitfall. Women read tone as an indicator of disposition, and therefore, a barometer on the *health of the relationship*. For males, tone is simply an attention-getter, and therefore, a barometer on the *importance of the task*.

Anson Dorrance says:

> "Through trial and error, I have learned that the women I have coached listen less to what I say than to how I say it. In other words, they listen less to the language and more to the tone. If my tone is negative, it doesn't matter how positive the words are. They are going to hear negative. If your body language is negative, it doesn't matter how careful you are in constructing your sentences to create a positive impression. It still comes out negative. Women listen to your tone and watch your body language, regardless of what comes out of your mouth." (19)

These tendencies develop early. A colleague with a young daughter was entertaining us with stories of her first season of soccer competition with her father as the coach. At one point in a game, the six-year-old girl came running to the sideline in tears. "Daddy's really mad. He's yelling at us," she sobbed. Angered that her husband would yell at a six-year-old, my colleague asked, "Well, honey, what did he say?" "He hollered that we had to try harder," the youngster whimpered. The message was innocuous but the tone had upset her.

I remember forcefully instructing one of my players during a match. I had called a timeout because my team was not following my game plan. I had the key player directly in front of me, and I was close to her face. I was speaking loudly, asking for repeated confirmation that she understood what I wanted her to do, and pounding my fist into my other hand. Finally, I asked aggressively, "Have you got it?" She nodded her head affirmatively, but then her eyes filled with tears. She said, "You hate me, don't you?"

I realized quickly that my delivery had distracted her from my words. Backpedaling, I put my arm around her shoulders and said firmly, "No, I don't. I just need you to do these things right now." She returned to the court somewhat comforted, but by her play, completely oblivious to my instructions.

Conclusion

Today, participation in athletics is viewed as a rite-of-passage activity for both girls and boys. Our expectations for what-we-can-be-when-we-grow-up have broadened, and our sports cultures have expanded to complement the change. Today, we are as likely to find girls as well as boys in the gym or on the field. Equal treatment for male and female athletes is now an assumed goal instead of the laughable pipedream of the past.

This sea change gives us an opportunity to evaluate our assumptions about the value of game playing in a larger social context. What we find is that sports is one of the few places where each gender can act out the other's script without the usual social consequences. Our rigid rules for gender behaviors seem to relax during contests.

For example, as part of a team, males are allowed to express themselves in ways that are unacceptable at other times—they may cry over a loss, they may hug each other in celebration, they may hold hands as a display of bonding, they may drape their arms around one another to show solidarity. These physical displays are permissible without penalty between male teammates. Further, males engaged in athletic contests are encouraged to sacrifice for others, to communicate verbally, and to cover for weaker teammates. While we usually don't identify them this way, these traits have traditionally been associated with femininity in our culture.

Females, on the other hand, are allowed to express the masculine side of their personalities during athletic contests. They are encouraged to show leadership, are praised for boldness, and are applauded for "taking charge." They are cheered for cold-cocking an opponent, dressing down a teammate, and outmuscling a rival. When engaged in sports, females are rewarded for behaviors usually associated with masculinity.

This timeout from our behavioral straitjackets gives both male and female athletes a unique opportunity to explore the full range of their human potential without pejorative sanctions. Sports may initially attract girls because of the social interaction, but if we do our jobs as coaches, sports will teach females to enjoy competing and being assertive. Athletics may initially attract boys because they like the competition, but to be really worthwhile, sports must teach males the benefits of attachment and empathy for others.

In the long run, the value of participation in sports has little to do with running, jumping, or throwing. The ultimate merit is in teaching females to appreciate battle and males to value bonding. At its best, sport teaches us how to be whole people and, thereby, prepares us for a more successful life beyond adolescence.

3

Gender Differences in Competitive Work

According to the Bureau of Labor Statistics, in 1960, 38 percent of women worked in the paid labor force. By 1997, that number had risen to almost 60 percent. From 1970 to 1993, marriages with two earners rose from 39 percent to more than 60 percent. In 1996, two-thirds (66%) of working women reported that they earned half or more of the family's income. (1)

Clearly, gender roles are changing. Today, men and women are often equal partners in financially supporting their families and jointly caring for their children. No longer is it just women who seek to "have it all"; now men do too. And just as women have struggled to find a balance between demanding work and responsible parenthood, now men do too.

The Detroit News recently reprinted a *Wall Street Journal* article entitled, "Men, women more alike study shows." Author Sue Shellenbarger says:

> "It's fashionable these days to highlight the ways—beyond the obvious—that men and women are different. … Now come workplace researchers telling us something really different: Men and women are a lot more alike than you may think.
>
> The time men and women put in caring for family and doing housework, their reactions to work-family conflict, the ways they want to structure work around family—all are growing so similar that seasoned researchers are flabbergasted … . [S]tudies show that men are actually changing their behavior. Most of the changes cut across demographic groups and encompass men in both single and dual-earner households, suggesting a mainstream shift among men toward greater involvement in nurturing." (2)

Work roles are also changing. Today, growing numbers of women are principals, men are elementary school teachers; women are doctors, men are nurses; women are pilots, men are flight attendants. Gender is slowly disappearing as a determinant in the workplace of adults and has already largely disappeared from the "what-do-you-want-to-be-when-you-grow-up" expectations of children.

Gina Bellafante made the following observation in a *TIME* magazine cover story on feminism: "... [T]he women's movement changed our individual lives and expectations, and young women today acknowledge this. A hefty 50% of those from ages 18-34 told the pollsters in the TIME/CNN survey that they share 'feminist' values, by which they generally mean they want a world in which they can choose to be anything—the President or a mother, or both." (3)

Does this apparent meshing of roles and expectations mean our distinctive group personalities will androgynize into a genderless generic? Anthropologist Helen Fisher says no. She claims that our biological roles and subsequent hormonal peculiarities guarantee our gender uniqueness. In her book *The First Sex*, she uses Darwinian logic to establish the biological basis of gender differences: "Men and women emerge from the womb with some innate tendencies and proclivities bred on the grasslands of Africa millennia ago. The sexes are not the same. Each has some natural talents. Each is a living archive of its distinctive past ... . These gender differences appear in cultures around the world. They reemerge decade after decade in the same society, despite changing attitudes about women." (4)

Further, Fisher asserts that the influence of this biological hardwiring is not likely to change. "Fewer women," she says, "are willing to sacrifice precious time with family to meet the grueling schedule and demands ... [some] jobs regularly require ... . This reality—women's *need* [emphasis added] to balance work and family—is central to understanding women's progress in every sector of the economy. It will continue to be crucial as the twenty-first century proceeds." (5)

Certainly, we are in a time of transition. Despite our innate biological differences, we are increasingly engaged in an economic dance where the lead is no longer based on gender, and the steps are unfamiliar. The cadence of our parents' lives was different from our own. For many of us, a predictable rhythm nurtured us from childhood into adulthood, making today's accelerated syncopation feel frighteningly out of control.

The stories of our competitive play can teach us. They provide not only unmistakable testimony to our gender dissonance, but also recognizable, emotional linkages to familiar situations. Success and failure in sport are obvious and public, making the lessons definitive and immediate.

Although this instantaneous feedback is absent in most workplaces, competition with others is certainly evident and routine. By examining our workplace dilemmas through the same lens as our playground dilemmas, we gain further insights into our gender idiosyncrasies and find means to improve our collective functionality.

A Lady into Fundraising

A story C.M. Newton, my former boss, loves to tell is of a discussion he had with a colleague regarding his intention to put me into the primary fundraising role in our athletics department. His promotion would make me the first woman in this position in the Southeastern Conference.

It was a Sunday afternoon and a well-meaning associate had caught him in his office watching a golf tournament on television. "Coach, are you sure you want to put Kathy into this job?" C.M. did not look at his intruder but continued to stare at the TV set across the room.

Sensing that the decision was not final, his colleague decided to make an argument. "Now, obviously, this is your decision, but let's think about it just a minute. Fundraising in intercollegiate athletics is nothing if it isn't good-ole-boy-ism. I mean guys get together, mostly to play golf, that's where the relationships come from, right?"

Coach Newton conceded, "Um, yes, I guess so."

"Alright, now let's think about your typical golf outing. A bunch of guys get together and right off start sandbagging, lying about their handicaps, and betting on who is going to win and by how much. That will be hard for a lady, don't you think? That's sure not how my wife plays golf. Then they start drinking beer and smoking cigars. Now come on, Coach, that's no place for a lady, is it."

Coach Newton responded with a noncommittal, "Mmm," indicating he was listening but not necessarily agreeing.

"Listen to me, Coach, you know yourself, it only goes downhill from there," his advisor implored. "Once they get a little tuned, they start telling dirty jokes and using profanity. How can you put a lady into that situation?"

At this point in the retelling, C.M. always starts giggling. He reports that he told his colleague, "Hey, listen, all that stuff is valid, but you haven't said anything yet that would eliminate Kathy." Then he howls with laughter and pounds me on the back.

The Importance of Winning

In the male world, accomplishment rules—it provides an objective measuring stick by which to judge performance in contrast to others. In the female world, community rules—it provides a subjective measuring stick by which to gage connectedness in contrast to others. Both are competitive cultures, but each culture measures success by its own standards.

Elizabeth Perle McKenna wrote *When Work Doesn't Work Anymore*, a book that describes and questions the appropriateness of our traditional workplace mantra. She says, "[The] rules for fitting in and succeeding [at work] are not just guidelines for success but the bones of a value system … . When we adopt the conventional picture of success, we are forced to live by its values. These values ask us to judge ourselves by our behavior, by our outsides and accomplishments. We become valued by what we do, not by who we are … . Because achievement was society's most important measure of a person's worth, this system makes no allowance for anything to be more important than work." (6)

When I chose coaching and athletics administration as a career, I wanted to achieve at the highest levels. I was determined to go places in organizations where I didn't see any women at all, much less women with children. I was already traveling two or three days a week on an irregular schedule. I always had responsibilities on weekends. I had chosen an occupation—intercollegiate athletics—that was more a lifestyle than a job.

To an extent, I am the product of an era. I grew up in a time when women were assured we could "have it all." Feminist rhetoric had convinced me that the barrier to female equality in the workplace had been simply blatant gender discrimination. Changes in laws, access to education, higher achievement goals, and an opportunity were the only things we needed to remedy workplace disparities.

What I found, however, was that after attaining an M.B.A., after setting high goals, after multiple promotions, I still had to deal with the issues of children and quality of life. I realized it was not as simple as straightforward *gender discrimination*. Life for me, as for others, was a series of choices.

Life with Matthew: A Story about Women, Coaching, and Kids

Life with Matthew actually began well before he ever appeared on the scene. For his unsuspecting parents, it began sometime in mid-February of 1988. It began for me about the middle of March. Mary, my assistant coach, came into my office one afternoon and told me she had just received confirmation that she was pregnant. Call it the 1-in-100 chance, call it another great failure of modern medicine, most definitely call it terrible timing, but she was pregnant and due in the middle of our next volleyball season.

I hesitate to admit our mutual reaction: Her coaching career in a Division I program was over. There was no way we could function with one of our staff out of commission at midseason, and, even if we survived that, how would we recruit, travel, or work our normal unstructured days, nights, and weekends?

The thought of losing Mary from coaching was, for me, a very painful one. She had all the "right stuff": She was an excellent trainer, she had a keen insight into the game, she had a knack for recruiting, and with six years of varied experience, she was invaluable to my program. She was a competent, qualified, experienced woman—the very characteristics administrators were seeking in candidates for volleyball coaching positions. And yet the fact that she was pregnant suddenly disqualified her in my mind and her own, and would do so in the minds of most administrators.

As we sat and talked, the hypocrisy of our reaction became increasingly clear. Here we were, two women coaches who had unabashedly supported the positions that women's teams should be coached by women if possible, that the field of athletics should be accessible to women at the elite levels, and that it was part of our responsibility to encourage, train, and promote women. We took those positions with complete knowledge of the time and travel demands of Division I coaching and, as we were both married, with intimate understanding of the stress that coaching puts on spouses. Yet when confronted with the possibility of risking our own program's success to support our convictions, we were both more than ready to accept traditional thinking.

Fortunately, for our program, by the end of the conversation, both Mary and I were not only convinced that we could take the risk, but were somewhat excited about it. Mary and her husband had planned to have a family someday, and I was more than happy to share their experiences vicariously.

Given our natures, it was only a matter of time until having this baby took on some of the characteristics of a competitive event. Our competitive instincts were fueled by the myriad of coaches, both male and female, who noticed Mary's expanding body, asked when she was due, and proclaimed us to be crazy.

The early signs that Matthew was on the way were fairly subtle and easy to adjust to unless, of course, you were Mary. She wore a path between her office door and the bathroom, as nausea was just a thought, suggestion, or smell away. Also, fairly early on, I lost my running partner, my junk food splitter, and my drinking buddy. In the gym, Mary soon stopped lifting the heavy poles in our net system, and she became reluctant about assuming the mid-court ball-tosser position, as that person routinely becomes the target for opponent's hitters. Other than that, our athletes never suspected anything before Mary told them she was pregnant in late April.

During the summer, Mary's body began to change more dramatically, and we noticed that she developed two new habits. First, she became excessively modest, always changing clothes in the bathroom stall, in her office with the door locked, or anyplace where no one would see her expanding physique unclad. Second, she started walking faster and faster, taking ever-longer steps. When questioned about this by those of us gasping to keep up, she disregarded it as idle teasing. Later, however, she admitted that she was in the habit of seeing her feet when she walked, and as her stomach grew, she inadvertently took longer and longer steps to accomplish this.

When the fall season started, Matthew was due in six weeks. I observed certain advantages to being or traveling with a coach in the advanced stages of pregnancy. For instance, in my nine years of coaching, none of my players has ever offered to carry my bags for me, yet they were more than willing to carry Mary's. Also, it became much easier for our group to make time through crowded airports; we simply put Mary in the lead. Her steps, by that time, were gargantuan, and people dove out of her way, clearing a nice path for the rest of us.

Matthew also unwittingly provided us with some great moments of entertainment. I remember one plane ride home when he was particularly active. Mary set several airplane peanuts on her stomach, and we watched to see how long it took for Matthew to kick one off.

Besides gaining comic relief, I think our athletes learned a lot from Mary's pregnancy—at least they sure asked a lot of questions. To her credit, she shared with them very freely, even some rather private details.

The drawback to traveling with a pregnant coach was the ever-present possibility of an early delivery. This was a thought our student trainer found horrifying. Mary's husband, Mark, also found the idea distasteful, since he harbored a good deal of competitive animosity toward some of our opponents and did not relish the thought of listing one of their hometowns on the birth certificate of his firstborn. Mary handled the situation on the road by carrying in her wallet the number of a local hospital and calling ahead to let the staff know she would be in town.

We did have one close call. The week before Matthew was due, we were to play at Texas and Texas A&M. Mary's doctor had cleared her to travel, but Mark, just to make sure he didn't miss anything, had decided to go with us. As he was the only coach (labor coach, that is) who knew the correct Lamaze breathing techniques, we agreed.

The day of the match, Mary did not act like her usual self: she skipped breakfast, sat through practice, and generally stayed to herself. Not wanting to alarm us, she said she simply felt sick and was sure it was something she had eaten. Actually, she was showing signs that labor was, if not imminent, certainly not too many days away. Her doctor had advised her by phone that she should go to the hospital for an examination.

After our arrival at the gym, Mary, Mark, and a fairly stunned Texas student trainer made a quick trip to the local hospital emergency room. They had been alerted that a pregnant woman was on her way, but, as Mary tells the story, they stared at her as if she were the first one they had ever seen. Once in the examining room, the attending nurse took on her most maternal tone and said to Mary, "You weren't really going to play tonight, were you, honey?" It seems that the panicky phone calls had led the emergency room staff to believe that they were receiving a collegiate volleyball player who had started labor during warm-ups.

As it turned out, the doctor assured Mary that she was simply experiencing some pre-labor symptoms and that the doctor "thought" she could finish the trip without a delivery. The doctor sent Mary back to the gym, and she was back on the bench by the start of the second game. The incident was enough to scare us, however, and Mary and Mark flew home the next day.

The following Monday, Mary was back in the office as usual. We were discussing the weekend's matches, which we had split, and complaining about our team's lack of serving ability. We needed to serve tougher and with more consistency if we wanted to achieve our goal of making the Final Four. I asked Mary to design some serving drills for that day's practice.

By this time, she was feeling huge, awkward, and constantly fatigued, so she put a chair at mid-court from which she could supervise drills. After explaining to the players what she wanted them to do, she went to her chair and lay down in it (you don't really sit anymore when you're that big). After all our encouragement, the first server went back and promptly served six balls into the bottom of the net.

Mary was angry. She bolted out of the chair, ran across the court, got face-to-face with the offending player, and let out a verbal tirade that was the culmination of our yearlong frustration with our team's inadequacy in this area. That evening Mary went into labor.

Matthew was born the next afternoon at 2:30. Signs appeared all over proclaiming his birth, including an "It's a boy" sign in *my* front yard. Several of our neighbors stopped by to congratulate us and ask if they could cook my husband a meal. Of course, he gladly accepted.

I'm not sure we could have survived a midseason baby had it not been for Mary's attitude and resilience. We had a match the evening of the day Matthew was born: Mary watched the tape in the hospital that night. By the weekend, she was back on the bench, although moving somewhat gingerly. In less than a week, she was back in the gym.

Because Mary chose to breastfeed Matthew, he became a part of all our lives for the rest of the season. He slept and ate in the office, he slept in the gym during practice, he slept behind the bench on road trips and with his dad in the stands during home matches. For those last two months of our season, I found Matthew's most appealing characteristic to be his need for lots of sleep.

Like most babies, Matthew adapted to breastfeeding very quickly. As long as food was available when he was ready to eat, he was happy. Mary, on the other hand, was not accustomed to being ruled by a biological clock, and could not always predict his feeding times.

In early December, when Matthew was six weeks old, we played our first NCAA Tournament match against the University of New Mexico. Several of our top recruits were on campus for the weekend, and Mary had taken them to dinner before the match. She had fed Matthew and left him with Mark with a bottle. About three hours later, we had won the second game of the match, putting us a game away from victory, and Mary a game away from relief. We lost the next two.

Mary was in agony. During the five-minute break, she rushed to the locker room and, manual breast pump in hand, locked herself in the bathroom stall. As usual, our team was oblivious to any problem and calmly won the fifth game 15-9.

Road trips with Matthew were an experience. He was generally well-behaved, pleasant, or asleep, but he single-handedly doubled our team's luggage. We needed the car seat, the rocker, the foldout bed, the diaper bag, four-days' worth of diapers, four sets of clothes and pajamas (in case of an accident a day), and a bottle for the plane (Matthew didn't chew gum yet). Fortunately, the team was more than willing to help transport Matthew; in fact, they would fight over whose turn it was to carry, rock, or play with him. Unfortunately, their maternal instincts departed when it came to carrying his luggage.

As Mary was generally overburdened with Matthew's luggage, she packed lightly for herself. This was not a problem until the evening of the Southeastern Conference Championship match—a television appearance for us—when Matthew had an accident on his mother's dress. After that, Mary always took a spare.

Matthew cooperated fully with our plans to win the Southeastern Conference Championship and get a bid to the NCAA Tournament; in other words, our season was not the dismal failure that we had feared and so many had predicted. Yet there were definite ways in which Matthew had made our lives more difficult.

I was amazed at how quickly Matthew realized that when his mother was in discussion with me, she was not paying attention to him. He responded to this affront by fussing. I took this very personally until I realized that the same thing happened when she spoke on the phone, and that his irritation was not directed at me. The good news is that this kept our discussions brief and to the point; there were certainly times, however, when he interrupted our workflow.

A more difficult adjustment was dealing with Mary's change in priorities, which affected Mark as her husband, me as her boss, and our players as her team. We were not always the most important people to her anymore. She certainly never ignored us or her job, but Matthew took a lot of her physical and mental energy, leaving less for the rest of us.

As I mentioned in Chapter 2, Mary moved on to the head coaching job at the University of Florida. I moved out of coaching into administration. But the questions for Mary, as a working mom, and for me, as the supervisor of other working moms, remain the same. We think we can arrange our work to accommodate children and their needs, but fool ourselves if we never have moments of doubt.

What happens when home and work conflict? What about when a woman has multiple children? How do moms handle their guilt when they're not home and how do bosses and coworkers handle their bitterness when mom is home? Basically, do moms have the time to succeed in competitive workplaces?

These are not unique questions; they must be answered by all women with young children who work outside the home. The difficulty is that few role models exist in intensely competitive professions.

We don't have all the answers right now. We know that "family" must be a viable option for women in coaching and other high intensity fields if we are to see a growth in the number of women choosing those careers. We also know that more and more women thrive on competitive events, so if there is a way to make it work, we will find it. (7)

The worldview that life is a contest produces a different set of standards from the worldview that life is a community. One engenders an every-man-for-himself ethos valuing workplace achievement as the ultimate benchmark. The other engenders a we're-all-in-this-together ethos valuing healthy connections as the ultimate scorecard.

Keeping Score

Keeping score, or avoiding it, is not confined to physical activities. At work, it means assessing where you stand and what you control.

In the male world of work, it is very easy to see the effects of life lived as a contest. Conversations are used as opportunities to spar, to hype an accomplishment, or to criticize a rival. Organizational charts identify reporting lines and span of control. Salaries measure value. The overt nature of the competition and the score makes it easy to identify and evaluate.

Women also assess where we stand and what we control, but we are more likely to do so through the guise of camaraderie than confrontation. Using the cloak that "this-really-doesn't-matter-to-me," women assess their wins and losses in relation to others.

Because women hate hierarchy, we have found ways to assert ourselves in clandestine ways. We subtly sabotage the boss by backstage bitching; we demurely derail an agenda by coffeepot complaining. We cannot appear blatantly concerned with who is ahead of us or behind us, but we are acutely aware of our place in the organizational configuration.

The difference between male and female scorekeeping at work is the overt versus covert nature of the activity. Males accept jockeying for position as part of the game, as an irrefutable function of workplace life. They may not enjoy the scrum, but fatalistically they engage anyway. Females want hierarchy to go away. We begrudgingly play the get-ahead game and punish each other and ourselves for our sensitivity to it. The incongruity of the game with our identity drives us underground.

Battling for Turf

Controlling decisions and/or resources is power in any organization. When I moved into a management position in our athletics department, I let several areas of responsibility shift to others in the interest of being a team player. Even though I did not judge these tasks important, my staff assistant reacted angrily. She had seen her former boss fight to control these areas. In my mind, these were insignificant little jobs that were time-consuming and thankless. I wanted to be rid of them. In her mind, turf was turf, and I should horde as much as possible.

The female predilection to flatten workplace structures, share decision-making, and push power down the organizational chart makes traditional turf battling, defending, and acquiring uncomfortable for us. Instead of the instinctive scorekeeping activity it is for our male counterparts, we must persuade ourselves that it is, at times, important and necessary.

In my fundraising role in intercollegiate athletics, men's basketball tickets were the most powerful tool. They were in short supply and, therefore, a valuable means to reward donors or magnanimously dole out special favors. Further, major givers were very conscious of where they sat in an arena and who sat in front of them. Early in my tenure, I learned that as trivial as these issues seemed to me, they were very important to the people I served. Out of necessity, I became more involved with ticket issues than I wanted to be. I realized that neglecting this "turf" was giving away power and influence that I needed to be effective.

Because turf battling is unnatural for women, we frequently miss the nuances of when to protect it and when to concede it. We had a female trainer in our organization who became publicly upset with a doctor when he accompanied her onto the basketball court to evaluate an injured player. She told the doctor that it was *her job* to make the initial assessment of the injury and that he should stay on the sideline until she motioned for his help.

The incident made her look bitchy and naive to the males in our organization. From their viewpoint, turf is ceded without question to a superior. Their food chain is vertically integrated and recognizing one's place in it is key to survival. From her viewpoint, the rebuke of the doctor was a legitimate defense of turf. The key to survival in a horizontally integrated group is to identify your specific role and then protect it from encroachment by others.

Applying for Jobs

Jockeying for a new job is another way to assess the score. By definition, it is a zero-sum activity—one person wins and everyone else loses—and therefore often more comfortable to males than females. For men, applying for a new job is often a "what have I got to lose?" proposition. It's a challenge, a mini-contest. It's risk-taking that has little downside and a lot of upside—a new job or increased leverage in your current job. Besides, they reason, an interview is always good practice, and just being "in the hunt" is a way of scoring. Qualifications? Why fret about that? Let those doing the hiring evaluate whether you're competent or not. For all these reasons, men more readily apply for jobs than women.

To women, the idea of engaging in a job hunt with a hidden agenda feels dishonest. Applying for jobs just to see where we stand, either in the job market or at home, is a type of head-to-head confrontation that seems repulsive, not playful or adventurous. Instead of seeing the upsides of a new opportunity—leverage at home, or points in future searches—we focus on the downsides of job hunting—less-than-straightforward negotiating, disruption of our personal lives, and the possibility of rejection.

When I became an athletics administrator, my former coaching colleagues sought my advice on a variety of work-related issues. Most wanted to know how they could increase their salaries in their current positions. I told them the fastest way was to have another job offer on the table. I said that for a few thousand dollars, most administrators would not go through the trouble of replacing a capable employee and that marketability equaled value in the athletics world.

I cautioned them that this strategy posed some risks. Their complaint was that they were underpaid by marketplace standards. By job hunting, they were choosing to test the truth of that claim. If they were wrong, if no one wanted to pay more for their services, they had lost whatever 'good guy' leverage they had at home. Further, I told them they had better be prepared to leave their current position. Their administration might decide to let them go to another job rather than feel blackmailed into a pay increase to keep them. Either way, I warned, the process was confrontational and often damaging to their relationships with their superiors.

Most of the male coaches thanked me for the advice, put their name in a few searches, went on an interview or two, and generally got a pay increase at home or a new job at a higher salary. They may not have appreciated the drill, but they participated in it as a part of the game.

The female coaches bemoaned the unfairness of this exercise. They did not want to fake interest in another job to be rewarded at home. They thought they should be recognized and compensated based on merit, not some feigned interest in going elsewhere. The disingenuousness disturbed them to the point that many chose not to play the game by the tacit rules I had given them.

The men were willing to play the get-ahead game regardless of their personal opinions about the rules. The women wanted to change the game and refused to play by the existing rules.

Elizabeth Pearle McKenna writes:

"Being a good worker does not guarantee success. Loyalty, dedication, excellence, and hard work without some form of self-promotion or some other way of being recognized often invite exile from the fast track. Because jockeying for position is more in line with the male mindset, men embrace this exercise as 'part of the game' more readily than women. … Every woman entering the business world soon finds that, contrary to her academic experience, how well she performs actually is only one factor in creating a future for herself. Instead, an unwritten set of rules directs her fate—a Darwinian system that weeds out those with no stomach for politics, competition, or monofocused ambition." (8)

The issue of what must be done to 'play the game' is usually a difficult one for women. Most of us come to the game with little experience in hierarchical structures and a different set of priorities and values from our male counterparts. More to the point, we respect our differences from men and consider our gender-specific ways of behaving and communicating as strengths that will improve our organizations.

Dealing with Failure

About four years into my coaching career, I interviewed for the head coach position at the University of Notre Dame. It was a job I was well-suited for and really wanted. My record showed I could build a program and, although I was young, I already had four years of head coaching experience to my credit. Besides, I was affordable.

They hired an older male coach with many more years of coaching experience. The decision crushed me. I blamed myself—thinking I must have blown the interview—and I mocked myself—questioning my sanity for even imagining I could get the job. I assumed the successful candidate had superior credentials and was a better choice. I decided that I had better just stay put and be glad I had a job.

Several months later, the University of Kentucky sought my services. Their former coach had quit in a very public quarrel with the administration over lack of support for her program. The University had hired a "name coach" from Hawaii to quiet the critics, but she had resigned two weeks after taking the job, creating another embarrassment. They needed to hire someone in a hurry. After a few panicked phone calls, they found me—young-but-affordable—rushed me in for an interview, and offered me the job. For years, I joked about myself as the candidate of last resort, and attributed my success in landing the job to their desperation.

Eight years later, one of my young male assistants applied for a job and lost out to a female candidate. He told me that he thought the interview process had been unfairly skewed in her favor, and that the only reason he didn't get the job was because he was a male. He never questioned his performance in the interview, which, I later learned, was abysmal, or the fact that he had relatively little coaching experience. He never mentioned that the successful candidate had superior qualifications as both a player and a coach, or considered that she might be a better fit for the institution. He blamed his failure on a flawed process and blatant discrimination, righteously absolving himself of any responsibility.

His reaction was so different from mine. He attributed his job loss to external circumstances outside his control. Although his failure to land the job frustrated him, it never affected his view of himself. From his perspective, he had entered a fair fight, and been cheated out of victory. Because his self-esteem remained intact, he quickly headed for the next contest. He continued to apply for jobs and eventually landed a position in a better program than the one that had rejected him.

Whereas my fear of failure overpowered my competitiveness, his competitiveness overpowered his fear of failure. I had internalized my failure, personalizing the rejection by accepting it as an accurate reflection on my competence. He had externalized his failure, labeling the rejection as structural and seeing no correlation to his competence. His ability to separate his failure from his self-esteem, to compartmentalize it outside himself, gave him a resilience I lacked at his age.

In competitive situations, the hierarchical mindset familiar to males is advantageous because it identifies and legitimizes the opponent in a way the web mindset does not. It has a defined adversary, an "other." This "other" is usually another person or group, but it may be a structural condition. Recognizing an opponent means competition can take place in an open format and without apology.

The web mindset, defining the world in the framework of connection, does not provide for a legitimate opponent. Head-to-head confrontation is discouraged, as is self-promotion and one-upmanship. For women, competing against another becomes a somewhat clandestine and often dangerous affair. Assertiveness must be balanced with cordiality, achievement with appropriate humility, and victory always tempered by acknowledgment of unworthiness.

No legitimate opponent means that the enemy for women all too often becomes the self. Instead of satisfaction with being "good enough," defined as better than the external opponent, we become obsessed with being perfect, judging ourselves against an internal standard that is routinely unattainable.

Self-Esteem

Many women athletes are perfectionists. I recognize the trait because I lived it myself. Downplaying strengths, deflecting praise, and denying compliments were all subconscious levelers and therefore means to acceptance in the horizontally integrated female world. You couldn't gloat or bask in the knowledge that you were better than someone else—it wasn't ladylike—so you adopted internal standards for achievement that kept your self-esteem in a constant state of siege.

I coached a poster-child perfectionist. Leslie was an excellent athlete—tall, strong, and relatively quick. She was a great player because she was both very skilled and intensely competitive, but she was impossible to coach. She could not stop beating herself up long enough to absorb any constructive criticism or corrective feedback. Her self-esteem was so fragile from regular internal floggings that any negative feedback crushed her.

She started as a freshman; broke almost every statistical record we kept; earned countless honors; and was named an All-American her senior year. Yet she was always miserable. When I praised her, she shrugged it off as vacuous flattery. When I corrected her, she sulked. When I criticized her, she fell apart. Even if she had played superbly, she focused on her mistakes or wallowed in some other inadequacy. Her lack of a legitimate external opponent sapped the joy of victory from her competitive experiences. Her opponent was always within, and always unconquerable.

I would love to report that I tempered my own perfectionist tendencies after I saw the debilitating effects on my female athletes, but I would be lying. I regrettably remember the joyless Calvinism I inflicted on the best team I ever had. I goaded them relentlessly with a that-was-not-good-enough whip. I only saw our weaknesses—my right-side player was young and inexperienced, one of my middle blockers had bad knees, we served the ball poorly. I obsessed about our vulnerabilities—my setter was a freshman, my defensive specialist was terrible, we did not receive well in rotation four.

My team was experienced, deep, and talented, but all I saw were our problems, mistakes, and shortcomings. We defeated many opponents rather easily, and more importantly, even when we played poorly, this group found a way to win.

We beat the number-six-ranked team in the country in their gym. Yet no victory, regardless of its significance, could convince me that we were better than average. We did not lose a match until almost midseason, yet I was convinced our success only reflected our weak schedule. My incessant faultfinding almost drove my best player off the team and created unnecessary angst for everyone involved with our program.

My constant bellyaching was not the closet narcissism so often heard from coaches—the we-are-really-terrible-but-are-winning-because-I-am-such-a-good-coach shtick. I was truly filled with self-doubt the entire season. Whatever we did, it was not good enough. I never shook the fear that we were really only lucky impostors. My team finished the season 31-2, but …

The Results of Competitive Achievement

Because most women have worked at the low ends of hierarchical structures, their difficulties with positional status may not surface until another woman enters the upper ranks of the organization. Traditionally, most men and women have accepted, although at times reluctantly, a pre-ordained, biology-is-destiny mindset. Women traded time with children for workplace power and professionally achieved status. As long as men held most of the positions of power in the workplace, the tacit assumptions remained largely unquestioned.

In this day and time, no one believes that only men can be bosses and managers and only women can be secretaries and receptionists, but the subconscious programming of history is powerful and real. Gender segregation has been such a pattern in our workplaces that it is often accepted and unnoticed until an "other" is hired.

When a woman enters a position in an organization where there have been only men, or a man where there have been only women, both incumbents and the new "other" hope that business will continue as usual. Frequently, however, the incongruity of the newcomer's gender role and his or her work role will raise communication issues among both female and male coworkers.

One of the Girls

Each gender shares tacit assumptions about appropriate behavior within its group, that is, women expect certain behavior from other women, and men expect certain behavior from other men. Gender ties us in terms of ground rules, perspective, and style of communication. In essence, gender links us even when our work roles separate us.

When I became the "first woman" at a particular level in our organization, the female staff assistants welcomed me, yet regularly reminded me that I was different from the men. If I came into the office after 8:00 a.m., their starting time as hourly workers, one of them would look at her watch and say jokingly, "Good afternoon," or "It sure would be nice to be able to come to work whenever you got around to it." These comments never accompanied my male colleague's routine 9:00 a.m. arrivals.

If I was out of the office for several days, which I was much less than my male counterparts, they would tease me upon my return by saying, "We didn't know if you still worked here, we see so little of you." On days where I was headed out with the guys to play golf, one of them would always say, "Wow, must be nice to play golf and call it work." Since I knew my management position gave me freedom they did not have, I never defended myself.

Forms of address in our workplace were Coach Newton, Mr. Ivy, and Kathy. Often, one of the female staff would say to me, "I don't want to bother Coach Newton or Mr. Ivy with this, but I thought you should know … ." They would come into my office, close the door, and share little, irrelevant, often divisive, tidbits of office gossip—confiding in me as if I shared their concern.

They teased me endlessly about leaving my poor husband home alone to fend for himself and not providing home-cooked meals for his sustenance. They praised him as the most long-suffering male they knew for his willingness to *let me* travel so much. They asked me when I ever found time to clean the house, buy the groceries, or do laundry. I never heard them question my male colleagues about finding time for these tasks.

These exchanges were never mean-spirited or hostile. The slights were unintended, the jokes innocuous, if tedious at times. I generally enjoyed the easy and friendly repartee that we shared, and willingly allowed myself to be the brunt of their jokes. They made a group project of finding appropriate clothes for me to wear to the Kentucky Derby and other formal functions that were part of my job. They good-naturedly mused that, "It takes a village to dress Kathy for a special event."

Our shared gender allowed us a degree of playfulness that was both gratifying and bonding. It was also much more casual than the relationship they had with their male superiors. During our morning time together before my male counterparts arrived, our interactions were often downright rambunctious. We talked too loud, hollering down the hall at each other, and often laughing hysterically.

My staff mischievously gave the code name KFPs to rigorous or tedious tasks I assigned them—K standing for Kathy's, the F standing for a ribald swear word none of them would ever use publicly, and the P standing for projects. When we were in a collective negotiation on a sticky subject and I showed disgust or impatience by closing my eyes or running my hands through my hair, one of my staffers would say to her counterparts, "She's getting mad at me; I'm getting that look." These women were not going to treat me like they would treat a male boss, even if I had wanted them to. No matter how high I rose in our organization, my rank would never transcend our connection as women.

Most of our assistants were women who had left the workplace or shortened their education to raise their children. By and large, they were smart, capable, and hardworking. Had they stayed in a career path or gained the requisite degrees, most were fully capable of doing my job or their respective bosses'. Their current positions were the culmination of choices made long ago. Their choices had nothing to do with ability and everything to do with biology, a fact long since forgotten by both them and their male supervisors. For both of them, in an innocuous way, gender and ability often melted into each other.

My arrival was both an affirmation of their potential and a reminder of the choices they had made. They were very proud of me, even if a little envious at times. Quite naturally, they also respected their own choices as legitimate. Some even felt their decision to sacrifice career for family was "natural" and "right."

Even when they acknowledged their choices, their low pay and lack of status in our organization often frustrated these hourly-wage women. They freely shared these frustrations with me. Initially, I think they thought I could improve their situations, and they felt I would because I was another woman. They soon found out I had more empathy than my male counterparts, but no more inclination or power than they had to change the status quo of our workplace.

Being conscious of the discomfort my presence as a manager might cause the hourly-wage women in the office, I was careful with my terms of address and introduction. I always referred to them as "assistants," never as "secretaries." Also, rather than giving orders, I asked for help when I wanted something done; I placed my own phone calls; and, thanks to word processing, spell check, and automatic formatting, typed much of my own correspondence.

I tried to organize our functions into interdependent, yet autonomous, areas, giving each worker separate tasks. I highlighted the fact that we were a team, that they knew more about much of our area than I did, and that each of us had to do our part for our sector to succeed.

I also worked relentlessly. I decided the only way to prove myself was to outwork everyone. I arrived at my office at 7 a.m. and rarely left before 7 p.m. I attended every athletic event I could fit into my schedule, and dragged my husband to so many social functions that we became known around our department as part of the "All-Banquet Team." I realized this strategy would eventually take its toll on me personally and professionally, but in typically female fashion, I could not think of another way to justify my position and salary.

I was very cautious when dealing with issues of rank. My boss was fond of working lunches. Usually, we went out to a local restaurant. Occasionally, time was short and he would ask the other associate and me to join him in his office. He would dig into his pocket for a twenty-dollar bill, give it to his executive assistant, and tell her to get us some sandwiches from a local shop.

My male colleagues had no trouble asking one of the senior staffers to make the lunch run, and from my observation, the women complied willingly. I sidestepped the task whenever possible. If unavoidable, I asked the senior assistant to find an intern for the task. On more than one occasion, I made the lunch run myself rather than ask one of the women. I felt as if I needed to keep my "pulling rank" chits, which I knew were limited, for more important things than lunch runs. Once, I even ordered a male assistant athletics director to "get us lunch" rather than ask a staff assistant. He knew I outranked him, and, accustomed to hierarchy and comfortable with the ramifications, he dropped what he was doing and headed for the sandwich shop.

Office Politics

Several times in our organization, one of our managers has attempted to re-organize a female support staff into a hierarchy. The thinking is that establishing a chain of command will increase the effectiveness of the unit. Each time we try this, a quasi-hierarchy is already in place, in that one member of the group outranks the others in grade and salary, and all in the pool are well aware of their respective gradations.

The attempt always fails. The lower-ranking women complain that they have lost their autonomy, that they have been demoted, and that they will not take orders from a colleague. Often, they transfer out of the unit, frequently into a similarly classified job. Regardless of their rank on paper, these women consider themselves a team of independently functioning equals.

Men and women think differently about status. Women are sensitive to status only when it is used to separate us from others, in which case we usually resent it; men are sensitive to status because it gives them the ground rules for their behavior within the group, and, therefore, they embrace it. In other words, women resent status because it is used to separate; men appreciate status for the same reason.

We employ a woman as a payroll clerk in our organization. She is capable, outgoing, gregarious, and well-liked by her colleagues. I asked her to join me in a meeting where some sensitive personnel issues were discussed. To protect those involved, I asked that the discussion be treated with strict confidentiality. About a week later, she said to me, "I really got worked downstairs about what's going on up here. People are mad at me because I won't tell them; they refuse to understand that I just can't."

The "people" she was referring to were her female counterparts. Their expectations of her as their friend included the open sharing of information and secrets. When she refused, they punished her, calling her "goody two shoes" and accusing her of being hoity-toity. She had to maneuver carefully between her peer group and me.

She was a valuable asset to me. I saw her almost every day, and, in our woman-to-woman chitchat that preceded or followed our work exchanges, she often shared informational tidbits that I would have had no other way of knowing. These helped me stay connected to a part of our workforce that I saw intermittently, but was expected to help manage. My male colleagues, who shared the same management responsibilities, had no such informal link to the morale of this sector.

The ground rules that women have for each other do not mesh well with a hierarchical structure. In fact, the we're-all-in-this-together of the web is the antithesis of the every-man-for-himself of the hierarchy. As long as only women are in the secretary/receptionist/office administrator positions and only men are in the manager/boss/director positions, the web of female relationships and the hierarchy of male building blocks coexist with minimal sniping. Each gender plays within its homogenous group by the rules of its own playbook.

The entry of a woman into historically male ranks—into the hierarchy—separates her from the other women in the organization. By position, she has moved outside their web. However, due to her gender, the other women in the organization will have difficulty interacting with her as if she were a man, nor would she want this. Her organizational role imbues her with a new status in the hierarchy; her gender role, however, keeps her uniquely linked to the other women in the organization regardless of their respective ranks.

The resultant misunderstandings are so predictable and pervasive that they have been codified into the gender stereotype that women undermine other women. I have heard this accusation repeatedly, read articles about it, and actually seen the results in the workplace lives of some of my female friends. Yet I never experienced this sabotage firsthand. In fact, my experiences have been quite the opposite—I feel tremendously supported, protected, and respected by my female assistants. Further, I have several close friends who are highly successful managers of other women. These incongruities make me question the stereotype.

Women Managing Women

From my observations, many women who are knifed by their female underlings received all of their formative management training from men. The schooling may have been excellent, but it gave these women no hints for adapting the lessons to their own gender. Maybe more insidious, their cross-gender apprenticeships never planted the seed that wholesale mimicry would not work.

My friend June is a most poignant example. June was a gifted volleyball player in a nationally competitive program coached by an excellent male coach. After graduation, she pursued a career in coaching. She spent three years working as an assistant for a male coach out West and three more years in an assistant's role under a male coach in the South. After her six years as an understudy, she was known nationally as an excellent recruiter, a tireless worker, a knowledgeable teacher, and an engaging personality. She was on everyone's short list of prospective head coaches. After protracted recruiting, offers and counter-offers, a major university finally won the bidding war for her services. Four years later, she was fired.

In reflecting on our conversations during her head coaching tenure, I now realize they had a common theme. June frequently expressed confusion, frustration, and resentment about her athletes. She made statements like, "I just don't understand them [her female athletes]. I do the same drills in the same manner with the same feedback as Bob [or Mike or Dave] did. They don't respond, they don't learn, they act as if they don't care." Or, "They complain that I'm too tough, too business-like. I'm not training them any differently than Bob trained us. He never tried to be our friend, and who would want that anyway." Or, "They say I treat them like men. Well, of course I do. I want them to get better." Or, "They turned on me as if I was the enemy. I've never seen such viciousness. Bob's [or Mike's or Dave's] players never did that to them."

June had no model of female leadership, nor would it occur to her that she needed one. Her mentors were all excellent women's volleyball coaches; they understood the game, knew training, and had figured out how a male effectively manages females. June could mimic their drills; she could mimic their training techniques; she could mimic their tactics; but she could not mimic their management style. Her female athletes would not allow another woman, regardless of her title, to manage them the same way they would a man.

This understanding was reinforced when I read Anson Dorrance's book *Training Soccer Champions*. Dorrance has many years of coaching experience with both males and females. Although his topic is soccer, the book is insightful and instructive for coaches of any female team sport. He opens a chapter entitled "Leading Women Athletes" with the statement, "You basically have to drive men, but you can lead women." (9)

The sentence caught me. I highlighted it and put a question mark next to it. It did not mesh with my experiences as a coach of female athletes. Dorrance is right that men respond to goading far better than women do, but his generalization about women's response to leadership did not ring true for me.

Could it be that female athletes respond differently to male coaches than they do to female coaches? Are women more readily led if the coach is male than female? I believe so. Dorrance's words must be paraphrased for female coaches to read, "You can *drive* men, but you basically have to *convince* women."

Look at the archetype success story of women coaching women: Pat Head Summitt. As the women's basketball coach at the University of Tennessee, she has won seven National Championships, more than any other program in women's basketball history. In March of 1998, *Sport's Illustrated* did a cover story on her entitled, "The Wizard of Knoxville," playing on the nickname, The Wizard of Westwood, given to the legendary men's basketball coach at UCLA, John Wooden.

One of the motifs that winds through the piece is about the relationship between star point guard, Michelle Marciniak, and head coach Summitt. In a particularly descriptive passage, author Gary Smith writes the following:

> "It's growing mutually, magnetically, their frustration with and affection for each other. If Michelle could just pigeonhole Pat as a tyrant, it would be so much easier. But Pat's the woman you wish you could cook like and water-ski like and chat up the cashier like and toss off one-liners like. Pat's the life of the party.
>
> How does she do it? How could she turn your name into an obscenity on the court, then walk off it and become your mom? How could a woman be transformed that completely, so that when you sit in her office, she leans toward you to connect with you, the flesh around those piercing eyes wrinkling in concentration, and invariably asks what you think the team needs and then, as you're getting ready to leave, asks if you think her beige shoes go with her white skirt. Not to con you or charm you, because you would eventually sniff that out. She asks so intently that it seems the two of you are the only ones in the universe, so honestly that you smell the unsure girl beneath the awe-inducing coach." (10)

Listen to the words Smith uses to describe Summitt: "woman you wish you could cook like," "walk off [the court] and become your mom," "unsure girl." These are distinctly feminine images. Change the gender of the coach to male and the meaning of the metaphors changes dramatically: "Pat's the *man* you wish you could fish like and fix the car like and tease your friends like and tell jokes like."

It is the unique femaleness of these exchanges that make Summitt available to her players, that connect them to each other. The rest of the article and any observation of Summitt in action dispel any notion that her coaching is soft, namby-pamby, or nurturing; yet her manner includes enough backstage openness, enough glimpses of tenderness, that her female athletes are convinced to follow her.

Women expect a particular decorum from other women. Regardless of the status differentials in the relationship, women need to see a hint of vulnerability before they will allow another woman to lead them. Can you imagine a writer insinuating that the phrase "you could smell the unsure *boy* beneath the awe-inducing coach" indicated strength in a male leader? The same trait—vulnerability—that would be identified as a weakness in a male leader is a vital link that convinces one woman to follow another.

Identity Issues

I often found myself somewhat self-conscious around the wives of the football and men's basketball coaches. Most of these women did not work outside their homes. Their husband's job required of him frequent relocation, 12-hour work days, weekend and evening hours, and unpredictable periods of time away from home. At the major college level, their husbands also made high salaries. The result was that many of their families were structured the traditional way—the male as the primary breadwinner and the female as the primary caregiver.

While my struggle was primarily to maintain my female identity in a world of men and work, their struggle was to establish their own identity apart from their spouses and children. Elizabeth Perle McKenna says in her book about women, work, and identity, "Earning money gives women power and freedom and an independent identity apart from a man or family. That earning capacity is the block from which self-esteem, a sense of purpose, and personal freedom are carved." (11)

I remember Carolyn Curry, the spouse of our football coach, telling me about the moment when she decided she wanted to "be somebody." She had been a stay-at-home wife and mother during her husband's NFL days, when they moved every six months between Atlanta and wherever he was playing. Then, she had wanted to stay at home when he began his college coaching career because their children were young and he was gone a lot.

Over time, her lack of individual identity started bothering her. One day, she was on her hands and knees scrubbing her kitchen floor. She said to herself, "Carolyn Curry, are you satisfied being remembered as a good wife and mother, and a woman with a clean house?" She decided to return to college and pursue a Ph.D. in women's history. She became an adjunct faculty member, writer, ardent feminist, and sought-after speaker on women's issues.

Most of the coaches' wives did not speak as openly with me as Carolyn did about their struggles for identity apart from their spousal roles. Their behavior indicated they felt they were doing the right things for their families, but they were living in a society where they were more often than not the exception rather than the rule. Most were college-educated with career potential, yet they collectively were swimming against the cultural stream that valued everyone, women as well as men, by the work they did outside the home.

I had more in common with their husbands than I did with them, and frequently our conversations never went beyond passing pleasantries. When they did, we often stumbled; I couldn't understand their identity struggles any better than they could understand mine.

One of the Boys

Do I Hold the Door or Do You?

My first few days as the only woman and the newcomer to a male team created some interesting dynamics. I was unsure of myself and eager to please. I thought the easiest way would be to mimic the behavior of my predecessor, at least in terms of exchanges within my primary work group. I was the lowest-ranking member of a three-person senior management group. My predecessor had been almost servile in his display of deference for our boss. He would jump ahead of him to open doors; he would run out to the parking lot and get the car—especially if it was inclement weather; when dining for business, he would handle the check before it ever reached the table; when traveling, he would load luggage and carry it to and from the car.

All these were simple acts of helpfulness and courtesy that I thought were worth mimicking. Besides, I wanted to avoid any circumstances where my gender might be an issue in our workplace. However, when I tried to perform these functions, I met with resistance or confusion. On my first day, the three of us were walking a short distance to another office on campus. As we approached the door, I jumped ahead to open it. As I tried to step out of the way so my companions could enter first, they both ran into me. One of them put his hand squarely in my back and directed me through the door in front of them. The other one said, "Knock that crap off." I think my act of deference had embarrassed them.

Several days later, I took my boss to the airport. I parked the car in front of the terminal and got out to help him with his luggage. He had three large pieces, including a set of golf clubs. I picked up the golf clubs and started into the terminal. He said in a stern voice, "Put that down. I can get it." Rather than allow me to help him, he struggled to find a way to carry all three bags at once.

I realized quickly that our workplace courtesies would be governed by gender rules rather than status rules. Since I was trying to fit in, I adapted quickly. I no longer tried to pick up the check. I no longer got the car or offered to drive. I opened doors and went through them rather than holding them. I offered to help carry luggage but was always refused. Since I was younger and more physically fit than my counterparts, I thought the game we played was patently ridiculous. But, since it was comfortable for them, most of the time I swallowed my irritation.

As would be expected, not all my male colleagues behaved the same way. Some followed the workplace rules, some the gender rules. Initially, our exchanges were confusing and a bit awkward; we would run into each other trying to hold doors or both hesitate expectantly; the waiter would end up with two credit cards or, at times, none at all; we would fight over luggage or both cavalierly leave it at the curb.

I took note of these petty rituals. Our sputtering through them was an innocuous yet ever-present reminder that we were different—not in any negative way—just different. The little rites had meaning; they contained tacit messages about courtesy and deference, as well as power and control. I clandestinely enjoyed tampering with them, watching reactions, seeing who got irritated, and observing who was clueless.

Honorary Manhood

Due in part to my gamesmanship, in part to my personality, I fairly regularly received "the compliment of honorary manhood." Males I interacted with bestowed on me the mantle of acceptance mainly when my behavior mimicked their own.

I was visiting one morning with a new donor who had decided to contribute a large sum of money to a new facility we were constructing. I had arranged the breakfast with him so he could meet one of our vice presidents and another high-ranking university official. The donor was speculating that it might be fun for the four of us to get together at his country club and play golf. As he was making tentative plans, he hesitated, saying, "Maybe this isn't such a good idea, I mean, you know, three men, one woman … all of us married …" Sensing his discomfort, the vice president jumped in and said, "Oh, you don't have to worry about Kathy, she's more 'one of the boys' than most of the men at UK." I quickly turned to the task of cutting my breakfast sausage into small pieces with a sharp knife.

My colleague was not trying to insult me but to put the donor at ease. I surmised that for him, high praise for a woman was that she did not stand out in her workplace as a woman, but blended copacetically with the men in the organization. Neither of the other men at the breakfast table flinched at the vice president's remark. Our conversation of a golf outing continued without interruption.

This was not the first time I had been "complimented" in this manner. After a presentation I did at a volleyball clinic, a visibly excited male colleague approached me and, in his exuberance, started pumping my hand. Like me, he coached a women's collegiate team. "That was great," he effused, "What super ideas!" I could see he was searching for an appropriate kudo. Finally, he blurted out, "You know what I like most about you? You know what makes you good? You coach just like a man!"

Another time, my boss and I were sitting in a meeting listening to a debate that had gone on for an hour. He turned to me and said, "This is a real pain in the ass." One of our other female staff members was sitting on his other side. She had heard him speak but not his words. In response to her inquiring look, he said, "This is a pain in the fanny." I laughed and asked him why he had changed his words. He whispered, "That's Betty, I can't talk to her like I talk to you. You're 'one of the boys.'"

I had mixed emotions about these "compliments." I had heard them often growing up as an athlete. People would tell me that I played basketball like a boy, or I served a tennis ball like a guy, or I hit a golf ball like a man. I had grown wearily accustomed to the association of competence in physical skills with males and incompetence with females. Although I relished the praise, I cringed at the innuendo.

To hear these comments coming from my workplace colleagues, unrelated to physical competencies, was unnerving. I naively thought that gender stereotyping would subside once we traded our tennis shoes and cleats for heels and wingtips. I associated it more with the playing field than the workplace, more with brawn than brains.

I found that the "compliment of honorary manhood" is just as prevalent at work as at play. Further, the intention is the same—flattery, an indication of acceptance, an affirmation that I had *made* the team, a congratulatory declaration that even though I was a "girl," I could be part of the club. As a youngster, because I could "throw like a boy," I was picked for the team. So, too, as an adult, if I was "one of the boys," I was accepted and respected.

Rolling with the Punches

Besides the pragmatic problems of male mimicry as a management strategy, a far more emotional issue for women involves our own gender identity. In our society, gender is a zero-sum trait—more manly means less womanly. The innuendo in the cliche "one of the boys" is "you are one of us."

Like most people, I craved acceptance, yet I did not want to negate my gender uniqueness. I was not one of them and, more importantly, I did not want to be. These intended kudos subtly insinuated that success in my work role meant failure in my gender role. I wanted to be perceived as strong, capable, and effective, but I had no desire to be perceived as manly.

One of the ways I managed this conundrum was with my dress. I wore a skirt and blazer, hose, and heels—always—every day—to every function. I chose traditional business attire in conservative colors, purposefully avoiding tight, low-cut, or revealing garments. My goal was to professionalize my image, while at the same time feminizing my rough edges. The routine was terminally boring, totally contrary to my more boorish nature, and counterculture for a woman in athletics, but it worked.

I attribute my first promotion at Kentucky to nothing more meritorious than my dress. Our athletics director at the time was a very private man who infrequently interacted with his staff. I had been on his payroll for two years when his only female administrator, my direct report, gained permission to take a leave of absence. His staff assistant called me and scheduled a meeting in his office. We had exchanged short hallway greetings four or five times during my two-year tenure, but had had little other contact.

He asked me if I would take on my departing superior's duties, along with my coaching responsibilities, for the year of her absence. I said I would and within five minutes he had dismissed me. On my way out the door, his assistant told me that I had been an easy choice for him because I always dressed so professionally.

My other strategy was counterintuitive—I was a hardcore feminist obsessed with body image. As aging took its inevitable toll, I became an exercise addict. I took my gym bag and work clothes to the athlete's weight room, arriving each day at 5:30 a.m. I ran, biked, and stair-mastered my body into cardiovascular fitness, and sit-uped and weight lifted my muscles into reappearance. The result looked more like an adolescent boy than a mature woman, but the combination of sinewiness, strength, and solitariness was empowering to me. I *felt* the daily discipline gave me stamina; I *believed* the routine gave me confidence.

I trusted my muscles to shield me against unwanted advances from men. "Make a move on her and she'll knock your block off," was a jab I considered wonderfully pragmatic. I am convinced my physicalness protected me to a certain extent. It removed me from the sphere of the datable, the harrassable, the ignorable, the walk-on-able.

Neither my choice of clothing nor my lean, flat-chested body type protected me from careless sexism, harmless regional colloquialisms, or hardcore bigotry. The challenge was quelling my automatic defensiveness long enough to fairly evaluate which was which.

In the fall of 1996, we hired a new football coach. I had been one of five involved in the final interview. We had prepared a recommendation for our advisory committee and were to meet for dinner after a reception for senior staff at the athletics director's house. The new coach's first greeting to me was, "How are ya, darlin'?"

I said, "Fine," but I didn't mean it. I liked this man and wanted him to respect me as a colleague. I desperately hoped his remark was simply provincial Southern dialect and not indicative of a condescending attitude towards women.

To counterbalance my first impression, I made a point to talk coaching with him, to be visible at his practices, and to always shake his hand firmly upon greeting, congratulating, or consoling him. Whatever his personal inclinations, he never referred to me as "darlin'" again and told me several times that he thought I would make a good athletics director.

The same vice president who "complimented" me on being "more one of the boys than most of the men at UK" also frequently referred to me as "hon." Several of our major male donors did the same, or used terms such as "dear," "doll," or "babe." I believe these terms of address were not meant to harm or insult. At times, I shrugged them off as simple expressions of familiarity and indications of friendship—the male equivalent of "big guy," "buddy," or "pal." At times, I seethed, passive-aggressively plotting a potent retort.

More than once, I warned myself to take counsel from a Rebecca Mark comment in a *Fortune* magazine article about successful businesswomen that "women need to try hard to roll with the punches." She said, "You can't take things people say personally. If you do, your confidence goes down, your ego gets in the way, and you don't get the work done. Then you're defeated." (12)

Some of what I read as "punches" was caused by regional and cultural biases in appropriate forms of greeting and touch. My stoic Dutch background, combined with my hair-trigger feminism, made me most comfortable with a firm handshake as the appropriate form of greeting with all but family and very close friends. Many males I encountered in the South were uncomfortable shaking hands with a woman and favored a triangular hug or even a kiss on the cheek or mouth. Many women also preferred a no-touch hug and a peck on the cheek to a solid palm-to-palm handclasp.

Initially, I cringed at this level of familiarity. I read the male touches as condescending and the female exchanges as disingenuous. I played keep-away from the male huggers and vice-gripped the tender hands of the ladies. Slowly, very slowly, I admitted to my Yankee prejudices, matured past my defensiveness, and adapted to the local customs.

Dealing with Dave

More than once, my brashness caused a Wile E. Coyote moment—I looked down and realized I had just run off a cliff. I was cocky about my ability to take care of myself and ended up in situations I should have avoided.

One of our major donors is a successful businessman in Georgia. He grew up in Lexington, Kentucky, and attended the University for a year before being drafted to serve in the Vietnam War. He finished college in Georgia, then worked for a major corporation for several years before deciding he could do better on his own. With a technically-oriented partner he started a mall development company. Dave was gifted, a risk-taker, and always on a mission to prove himself.

He made no secret of his love of booze and attractive women. Fortunately, I was not his type—I was not young enough, well-endowed enough, nor pretty enough—yet I had the access to high profile people and events that Dave craved. He adapted to me by treating me as "one of the boys."

On a visit to Lexington, he came into my office with a videotape he had made for a promotional event. It was predominantly footage of beautiful, busty women in skimpy bathing suits striking seductive poses. I did not know why he was showing the tape to me, as it was obviously produced for male ogling.

He asked me, "Well, what do you think?" I hesitated, not knowing what to say. I shrugged and said, "It's OK, I guess. Who's it for?" Sensing my discomfort, he said sheepishly, "I guess I should show this to the guys, huh?" Although this moment was a bit dicey, I vastly preferred my "one of the boys" status with Dave to the alternative.

One summer, he hosted a luncheon for our football coach in Savannah. As per his style, the event was staged in one of the finest hotels, complete with expensive wine, filet mignon, and a string trio for background music. Dave sat at a table with "a few of his employees," all of whom were gorgeous, twenty-something females.

By the time lunch was over, Dave was drunk. He gave his credit card to a busty brunette and told her to go buy herself a new bathing suit and to meet him at his pool later that evening. He and I retired to the bar, where we shared another bottle of wine.

By this time, I had no inclination to drive my rental car to the airport, but I was too cheap to take a cab and deal with the consequences. Dave took over my dilemma. He called the car company for me and told them the car would not start and they would have to pick it up at the hotel. Then he ordered a limousine and yet another bottle of wine. When the driver came in to announce he had arrived, Dave paid the large bill and joined me for the ride to the airport.

Quite quickly, I realized I had put myself in an untenable position. Dave had graciously and extravagantly hosted the entire day, solved my car problem and, now, to use a male cliche, he had "drunk me pretty." He reached over and tried to pull me toward him, saying, "How about just a little kiss?"

I put a forearm squarely in his chest and said firmly, "Dave, let's not go there."

He hastily regained his manners, apologized, and moved to his side of the limousine. The rest of the ride we returned to our usual repartee—sports talk.

I vowed to be more self-sufficient and avoid compromising situations. But I was also thankful for my "one of the guys" image with Dave. He wasn't looking for a struggle and the combination of my forearm shiver and our work history adequately doused his alcohol-induced amorousness.

The Meaning of Team Player

The mindsets of hierarchy and web lead to different concepts of team play in workplace settings. When men say that someone is a team player, they mean that the person is willing to accept their role in the structure, follow orders, and do their part even if, in the short run, it is not in their individual best interest. When women say that someone is a team player, they mean that the person is helpful, friendly, and shares the spotlight with others.

The differences are subtle, but significant. Men place more value on efficiency; women place more value on cooperation. Males choose teammates who can contribute; females choose teammates who can get along. Both characteristics are important to the success of a team and the lack of either can undo the most talented group. Where gender differences show up is in the importance placed on each.

Donna Lopiano, the Executive Director of the Women's Sports Foundation, shares this story:

> "Take a class of fourth graders and propose a game of kickball. Choose one boy and one girl in the class, make them team captains, and ask them to alternately choose their teammates. The boy will use his first pick on the best kickball player in the class; the girl will use her first pick on her best friend. The boy will choose the next-best available player with his second pick; the girl will consult her best friend and together they will choose one of their other friends with their second choice. The boy will continue to select his team by skill; the girl(s) will continue to select their team by friendship. The boy captain's team will win the game; the girl captain's team will laugh and have lots of fun."

If She Can Play, She's In!

One of my first days in the mostly male world of athletics administration, I had a discussion with a colleague about attending a golf outing. Because my main role was fundraising and because I was new, I knew every contact I could make would be helpful. Besides, I loved to play golf.

My colleague was very hesitant about including me in the outing. At first, I thought he was concerned about my golf, worried that I would hold up the play. I started to defend my skills, admitting that I had little finesse to my game, but that I could compete with many male golfers.

He assured me that he had heard rumors of my "grip it and rip it" style and that my game was not the problem. He said that this sort of outing was "a guy thing" and that the issue was not so much *my* comfort level but that of the male participants.

I was concerned. How could I possibly succeed if I were to be excluded from every "guy thing"? People likely to give to our programs loved sports both as spectators and participants. Especially because of my gender, I had to be a player rather than a bystander.

As it turned out that day, I was invited to play. There was a last-minute cancellation and, in order to make even foursomes, another player was needed. I won the longest drive contest, and my team finished second in the scramble. From that day forward, my gender was rarely an issue at golf functions. Once the guys found out I could help their team win, I was not only a regular, but a sought-after, playing partner.

For the male world, productivity is primary. You earn your place on the squad by performance, and you lose it by non-performance. When I was a junior in high school, I was invited to play on the boys' tennis team. The school did not have a girls' squad, and the coach knew I was a better tennis player than several male members of his current team. He was competitive and, even though I was a girl, he figured I could help them win a few more matches.

I was extremely hesitant. I knew I was better than some of the boys on the team, but I also knew that losing to a girl in an athletics event is worse than death for a high school boy. One of my male cousins convinced me to be his doubles partner. The doubles setting mitigated some of the *mano a mano* effects of my participation and was therefore more palatable to the boys on the team and to me. We played number one doubles and won more matches than we lost. When it became clear I could help the team win, no one on our squad questioned my participation. My competence earned me a spot on the team in spite of my gender.

My stockbroker is a vice president in a major company. Years ago, she entered the profession as a divorcee with two children to support, and as the first woman in her office. She had no formal training or prior experience. She was patronized, patted on the head, and mostly ignored until she became one of the top brokers in the firm. Suddenly, she was respected and consulted. She had made the team.

To describe the male world as a strict meritocracy is not only naive, but incorrect. Access, opportunity, feedback, and camaraderie certainly play a role in success. But productivity is such a highly valued trait among males that it will frequently supersede other barriers to membership in the group.

When to Speak Up

The tolerance of dissent is greater in flatter management structures. Diversity of opinion is encouraged rather than suppressed. Food chain positions are observed, but minimally. Since most women prefer to make decisions by collaboration and consensus, they will frequently create flatter structures.

When a woman manager asks her subordinates for feedback, she expects to get it. Those who simply regurgitate the "party line" are more susceptible to criticism than those that share independent thoughts.

In more rigid top-down structures, requests for feedback can be more an invitation to agree with the boss than a search for diverse opinions. If the "party line" is already determined, then those who dissent may be viewed as malcontents even though they have been asked for their thoughts. Accustomed to more hierarchical systems, men often assess the positions and personalities and adjust their behavior more quickly than women. At the very least, they will remain silent until they are sure their input is truly welcome.

Comfortable in a more amorphous structure, women have not always understood these nuances of structure. We bring to the office a Pollyanna naivete that has us convinced our opinions are valued and that it is our responsibility to share them, whether they are sought or not. Further, we assume those listening appreciate that our suggestions are only meant to help improve our organization or situation. We are flabbergasted when this seemingly innocuous behavior brands us as "difficult" or "hard to work with."

A very capable woman works for us in our academic services area. She was sharing a personal frustration with me one day. She said that in her staff meetings, the three male academic counselors for the football team often raise legitimate problems and concerns. However, when they get in meetings with the head coach and his staff, the counselors sit mute. She told me, "I just speak up. I don't care if they don't want to hear these things or if they get mad at me; these are problems they need to know about."

She could not understand the hesitancy of her male counterparts, nor they her outspokenness. She viewed their behavior as sycophantic and cowardly; they viewed hers as naive and foolhardy. Her instincts told her to engage the new coach as a teammate and quasi-equal; their instincts told them to lay back and assess the role they would be expected to play.

Her predominant team image was of a network of distinctively trained people, each contributing their expertise toward a shared goal. This perspective meant she gave little thought to power differentials between and among them. Their primary team image was of a hierarchy of positions and roles, each valued according to rank and status. That perspective meant they were acutely aware of power differentials between and among them.

The Nature of Contests

Women frequently struggle, particularly as newcomers, with the workplace assumption that "the job" is primary, and all else, including "getting along," is secondary, or possible only through "finishing the job."

Working for a Screamer

A friend of mine went directly from college into the high-pressure world of television news production. She was one of the first women on the crew at a large station in Denver. As in most major markets, the competition between stations was cutthroat. Ratings were a constant scorecard that translated into success or failure in advertising dollars. During the news show, the stress level was intense; all shots were live, timing was critical, and mistakes were obvious to millions of viewers. During the broadcast, the producer routinely screamed at his crew through their headsets; he called them names, attacked their characters, and swore at them.

When the show was over, everyone relaxed together over a cigarette and a beer. The abuse was accepted as a necessary component of the activity and, therefore, the male crew members never took the criticisms personally. Once the stress ended, workplace decorum returned, and all efforts turned to the evaluation of the day's performance and preparation for the next newscast.

My friend reported that most women did not survive, much less flourish, in this environment. They agonized over the mid-show criticisms, internalizing the negative feedback and blaming themselves for mistakes. They resented the screaming and name-calling, considering it unnecessary and unproductive. They separated themselves from the post-show camaraderie, unable to immediately forgive and forget the daily mayhem. The men on the crew believed women in general lacked the self-confidence and toughness to do the job.

My friend not only survived but thrived. In telling of her success several years into the business, she credited her participation in sports. She reported that the stress of news production was very similar to the stress of an athletic contest—everything was on the line, there was no second chance, decisions had to be made quickly, and players had to respond immediately and without question. Although not always comfortable with it, she had learned that the hollering and screaming was in the interest of winning, and, therefore, justified in that setting.

She said that, like her coaches, the top producers were perfectionists. They agonized over every detail of a show and punished themselves and their crew for every mistake. They dreaded failure much more than they enjoyed success. This made them temperamental, demanding, and overbearing, but it also made them good at their jobs.

Because she could "take it," she moved up quickly in the workplace hierarchy. She was viewed as a "tough cookie" by her male counterparts, and welcomed as "one of the boys." She truly enjoyed her work and was proud of her hard-won status, but she admitted to me that she was also lonely at times and yearned for the company of other women.

When a new woman came into her workplace, she befriended her and tried to teach her "the ropes." She said most women had had no competitive experiences that mimicked this environment, and, therefore, had no frame of reference for dealing with this kind of performance pressure. The tacit rules of this workplace culture about contests, acceptable rules within them, and success orientation were completely foreign to them. Many left quickly, unable to deal with what they defined as an abusive environment.

The "whatever it takes" attitude toward task accomplishment is identified more with males than females because, for males, winning is so closely tied to self-esteem. A hierarchical structure, by definition, rewards one-upmanship, blesses the conqueror, and deifies the top dog. Females, operating from a different perspective, find their greatest personal fulfillment in successful interactions with others, regardless of whether these interactions take place in the context of winning or losing. Success and failure certainly affect women's self-esteem, but they are defined in the guise of connection and are, therefore, inextricably linked to successful relationships.

It's Only a Game

My husband, Mark, and I have said to each other more than once, "I don't know what you are so upset about; it's only a game." Predictably, we say these identical words in response to very different circumstances.

One of our early battlegrounds was golf. We both enjoyed the game and had fairly equivalent skills. Since we also had mutual friends who played, we spent a good deal of our social time together on the golf course.

The battle generally began after my husband hit a bad shot. He would pound his club into the ground, often swearing profanely. His complaining continued through the hole and beyond, forcing everyone in the foursome, particularly his cart partner—usually me—to listen to him dwell on his error. If I were winning, his behavior was even more egregious.

If I said something in an effort to calm him, to cheer him, or just get him to lighten up, he snapped at me. In response, I retreated into smoldering, sullen silence. I viewed his poor behavior as his way of gaining a psychological edge. I thought it was unfair, intentionally distracting, and completely unnecessary. Frequently, by the time we had finished a round, I was angry and sulking.

Despite these mini-tantrums and my discomfort with them, he loved to play golf with me. He valued the time together, he enjoyed competing, and he loved the good-natured teasing and camaraderie that was part of the play.

For him, win or lose, once the round was over, it was over. He saw his anger and our hostile exchanges as part of the contest and, therefore, as exempt from the rest of our life together. After a round, he would cheerfully invite me to share a beer or offer to buy me lunch. When I sullenly refused, he would say, "What are you so upset about; it's only a game." From his perspective, I was taking his behavior during the contest way too personally. I was taking ownership of his frustration in a manner that was completely inappropriate. But his caustic rebukes hurt me and left me feeling bewildered, as if his mistakes on the course were somehow my fault.

Another activity we shared was watching University of Kentucky men's and women's basketball games. We both loved basketball. We had competed and coached, and we loved watching others do the same. I was connected to these programs through work; he was connected through his interest in sports, his employment at the University, and his desire to spend time with me.

I was a relatively quiet spectator. I cared deeply whether we won or lost and certainly had a vested interest in our success, yet my role was to support the team in a positive manner. Further, I had been on that floor and on that sideline; I understood the challenges, the feelings of vulnerability, and the pressure. My empathy for our coach and players was proportional to my memory. I celebrated the victories and agonized over the defeats, but I kept myself under tight emotional control.

My husband, on the other hand, was a very boisterous spectator. He freely shared his opinions about the play with those around him. A poor call by the official or an obvious blunder by a player could send him into a red-faced rage. If we were watching the game at home, he would scream at the television set, loudly cursing the offender.

One player on our men's team, Jared Prickett, was a good player, but now and then he would miss an easy shot near the basket. My husband would scream, "Jesus Prickett" whenever he bobbled a gimme. I loved to tease him during these mini-tantrums, "Dear," I would say, my voice dripping sarcasm, "I think his first name is Jared." His response to my joking was to sink into a smoldering rage and, as often as not, to leave the room for the television set in the basement.

If we were in the arena, he was somewhat more subdued. He would, however, carry on a snarling monologue under his breath about how poorly we were playing, how we did not have a chance to win, or how we were getting screwed by the officials. When I would debate him on a criticism or ask for more civility and optimism in his spectating, he withdrew into hostile silence.

He found nothing unusual about his spectating behavior, and, listening to other fans around the arena, I had to agree that he was not alone in his contest-induced insanity. Yet, the intensity of his emotion continued to baffle me. His dual obsession with winning and fear of losing leaked out of him as judgmental know-it-all-ism, destructive criticism, and pointless pessimism. More than once I said to him, "What are you so upset about; it's only a game." From my perspective, he was taking the contest way too personally. He was taking ownership of the outcomes in a manner that was completely inappropriate. But my sarcastic comments hurt him and left him feeling bewildered, as if his right to care was being stolen from him.

Over time, we adjusted to each other. Sometimes that meant holding our sharp tongues; other times it meant avoiding volatile situations. We still play golf, but frequently ride in different carts; we still spectate, but often times from different parts of the arena. Call it a copout if you will, but accommodating each other's quirks became easier than trying to change them. After all, at issue was only a game.

Fair Play

Most males define as fair and legitimate any behavior or tactic allowable "within the rules." Their worldview of competition encourages them to look out for themselves and to expect the same from others. They might *wish* for equal treatment, but they rarely expect it.

Males are generally more fatalistic than females regarding outcomes, crediting neither another's talents nor their own shortcomings, but blaming the system, politics, or favoritism. They spend little emotional energy on fairness, but rather focus on gaining an edge and retribution.

Women are emotionally wedded to fairness. Our worldview of interconnectedness and mutuality engenders concern for equality and impartiality, and leads us to expect that of others. Females narrow the definition of fairness by including deference to gender-related norms as part of the rules. Particularly in dealing with each other, women assume a mutual set of ground rules about appropriate behavior. These include communication with peers about motives and intentions, concern for group chemistry and other's feelings, and expectations that all will be treated equally.

Different Views of Fairness

Several years ago, our football team was losing. The head coach had to make changes on his staff to convince his superiors and the public that improvement was possible and to save his job. He targeted the recruiting coordinator and the strength coach. Both of these men were loyal, hardworking, long-term employees with excellent credentials and reputations. The recruiting coordinator was fired; the strength coach had his pay cut by one-third and was reassigned from the football team to the gymnastics, baseball, and track teams.

Neither of these men was singularly responsible for our failure. Yet, changes had to be made and they were singled out. Neither of them protested publicly about their plight or ever spoke about the fairness or unfairness of the decisions. They dealt with their feelings privately and quietly, and moved on to their next assignment. They understood the game, and accepted that their dismissal was "within the rules."

Contrast this situation to a changing of assignments in another campus department. One of the employees in that department resigned to take another job. Although her position was at the same grade as the other three positions in that department, several of the other clerks were eager for a change of assignment and wanted to be considered for her job.

A day after the resignation, one of them, named JoAnn, went to the male supervisor and asked to be transferred into the vacant position. He said the position would need to be posted, but that she was his first choice for a replacement and he would start training her immediately.

His decision created chaos on his staff. Another of the clerks, named Kim, had been sick that day and, when she returned, she was furious. Her anger was directed primarily at her colleague JoAnn. She told me, "This is so unfair. I would never have done this to her. I have more seniority than she does and she totally undermined me by asking for this job while I was away. She only thinks about herself. I can never work with her again."

I asked Kim if she really wanted the other job. She said that was not the point. The fact that JoAnn had not asked her whether she wanted it amounted to treachery and dishonesty that would impact their relationship forever.

I pointed out that the choice of successor was ultimately her supervisor's, and the timing of requests was really irrelevant. She said he had always taken advantage of her so she expected little fairness from him, but that she thought she could count on her coworkers for decency.

I heard from the supervisor several days later that his office was in turmoil. In his reassignments, he felt he had made the best choice for his sector, but the in-fighting had caused a virtual work stoppage. At the end of the week, JoAnn came in and resigned, saying she could no longer tolerate the hostile treatment she was receiving from her disgruntled colleague.

These women were struggling with issues of fairness. Their "play by the rules" treaty with each other had been violated by the lack of communication. Further, the supervisor had made a decision without consulting or informing everyone, a "within the rules" prerogative he assumed he had, but his female employees resented.

Pat Heim comments, "... men and women come into business settings with different approaches to doing the 'right' thing. For men, acting correctly means doing whatever it takes to achieve a goal; for women, it means doing what's fair to all. Because these motivations are so central to us, we frequently don't notice that our colleagues are working from a different frame of reference." (13)

Motivation

A friend named Ann is a very successful stockbroker in a large, well-known firm. She related a story to me about her first month as the number one broker in the office. Ann was proud of her success, having entered the mostly male profession as a rookie only a short time earlier. Her boss gave her a brief and very perfunctory "atta boy" and then proceeded to tell her how talented and hardworking the number two salesperson was and how difficult it would be for her to stay number one.

In the weeks that followed, the boss dropped little competitive teasers to both Ann and her colleague. He went to each of them separately and talked down the other, telling them how they could individually get an edge. The boss turned what Ann considered a collegial friendship into a zero-sum contest, pitting the two brokers against each other, creating a "winner/loser" mentality in their workplace.

This made Ann very uncomfortable. She held no malice towards her colleague and felt the boss was making "being number one" or "winning" way too important. She valued her relationship with her colleague and resented the distance the competition put between them. From her perspective, persistence, careful listening, a lot of hard work, and a little luck had carried her to number one, not her desire to beat somebody.

She withdrew from interactions with her office colleagues. The dog-eat-dog environment sapped her energy. As the only woman broker in the firm, she had no kindred spirit with whom to compare notes. She continued to work hard and produce good numbers, but she avoided engagement in the workplace politics. She thought of herself as a team player, but heard she was not perceived as one.

After some years, she made partner, and eventually was promoted to vice president. Only then did she realize that what she had perceived as unnecessary harassment was her boss' attempt to motivate her. She saw him repeat these tactics with young brokers and, if they were male, she saw it work.

She realized that her boss had assumed she shared his worldview. He saw his words as motivating; he was "throwing down the gauntlet," challenging her pride, he was, albeit inappropriately, appealing to her *manhood*. According to his mindset, everyone's primary goals were to make "top dog" and fight off challengers once they got there. Camaraderie and collegiality never entered his mind as motivators for achievement. Instead of building the relationships between his brokers, he actively disrupted them.

Feelings, caring, and warmth are not discussed very often in the context of competitive environments. For women, however, they may be critical components for success. Because the rewards for competitive achievement are greater for males, and relationships are more important to females, the absence of camaraderie will have a more negative impact on female competitors than their male counterparts. It's the companionship as much as the success that gives the activity value for women.

Tara VanDerveer wrote a book called *Shooting from the Outside* about coaching the 1996 women's Olympic basketball team to a gold medal in Atlanta. Her book details the year the team spent together, following their exploits from the selection process through the medal ceremonies. Although VanDerveer is a veteran coach, she describes the epiphanic impact the team's closeness had on her:

> "I was beginning to understand the power of feelings and of being positive, of tending to your players' souls as well as their minds and bodies. As important as X's and O's are, the players don't really care what you know. They just want to know that you care. I'm not so sure feelings are such an important element on a men's team, but for women, how they feel truly matters. I was coming to the belief that how they feel can dictate how well they play." (14)

Scream, but Say Something!

I learned a lesson about feedback from a player I coached named Sheila. She was a gifted athlete, but never became "a player." The mental parts of the game of volleyball—the anticipation of an opponent's tactics, the givens on what to expect in certain situations, the confidence to succeed in stressful moments—never became skills in her repertoire. The longer she played for me, the more frustrated I became with her lack of improvement. Her failure to progress was a negative reflection on my coaching, and I took it very personally. She was so physically gifted, yet so inept on the court.

She became my whipping girl. I constantly yelled at her, angrily corrected her mistakes, and punished her miscues. One day, after a particularly bad practice her senior year, I was struck with the futility of my own behavior. Sheila was improving only marginally, and I thought we were both leaving practice feeling bad every day.

I sat down with my assistant coaches and asked them to provide more feedback for Sheila. I told them I thought my constant badgering was unfair to her and that I hoped she would progress quicker with different motivation. I said I was going to break my habit of negative feedback; if I could not say something positive to her, I was going to be quiet.

Two days later, her voice quivering, Sheila asked to see me after practice. As soon as we sat down, she burst into tears. "You've given up on me," she sobbed. "You don't believe in me anymore." I said I was trying to give her a reprieve from my constant criticism. I told her that I thought she might improve quicker with a different feedback cycle.

She would not be consoled. "No, that's not it," she wailed. "You don't think I'm ever going to be any good." I tried to assure her that this was not the case, but until I promised to return to my cranky nitpicking, she heard none of it.

For Sheila, the absence of feedback was more devastating than negative feedback. My badgering was a sign that I cared, that I thought she could perform better, and most importantly, that I expected her to. When my nagging ceased, she noticed immediately, and she interpreted my silence as indifference about her chances for improvement.

I would love to finish this story in a *"Chicken Soup"* kind of way, telling you that after our meeting, Sheila became a great player, following my every instruction and dominating opponents; and that I found a much more productive, non-abusive way to motivate not only her but all of my future players.

Unfortunately, the true ending is much more ordinary. Sheila finished her career as a good player who never really lived up to her athletic prowess; I finished my career as a good coach who sometimes succeeded and sometimes failed as a motivator and a teacher.

But Sheila taught me something very important that day. She taught me to fear apathy more than anger in myself and others. Those who are angry still care, those who are apathetic don't.

I have noticed this same anger/apathy phenomenon with some of my staff. When I interact with them only minimally for a period of days, my primary assistant thinks she has done something wrong. More than once, she has come into my office and asked me if I am satisfied with her work. At first, her question confused me. I saw my male colleagues go for weeks without more than perfunctory exchanges with their staff. Now, I recognize it as a request for interaction. Like Sheila, my staff assistant read silence as indifference. Although she did not like negative feedback, she even preferred that to none.

My male staffers did not visibly suffer from a lack of feedback. Our male marketing director told me, "I figure if you don't say anything to me, I must be doing fine. If I screw up, you'll tell me." He read my silence as an endorsement of his work. His no-news-is-good-news perspective bolstered his confidence to act independently and take certain risks.

Responses to Authority

Whistles and Power

My 15-year-old nephew came to our campus for a week of boys' basketball camp. My husband and I went to the gym in the evenings to watch him play. One evening when we arrived, all one hundred boys were sitting on the floor waiting for a coaches' powwow to end so they could play.

After about ten minutes, one of the coaches stepped into the middle of the boys. He blew a short, shrill blast on his whistle. Most of the boys hurriedly got up. Once they were standing, the coach hollered at them, "Not fast enough! Sit down!" They all sat down. He blew his whistle again. This time they all scurried to their feet. "No good!" he bellowed. "Sit down!" When they were again seated, he snarled, "If you ever want to be any good at this game, you must learn to follow instructions exactly and immediately."

He prowled among the sitting boys, glaring at them for a moment. Suddenly he roared, "Stand up!" About half of the boys jumped to their feet. "You stupid sons of bitches," he screamed, his face turning red, "you're not supposed to stand up when I say 'stand up,' you're supposed to stand up when I blow the whistle. Now sit down, you idiots!" Obediently, they sat down.

I could see some of the boys rolling their eyes or snickering into their hands, but their protests were carefully hidden from the whistle-happy coach. At the next toot, all the boys jumped to their feet in chorus. They were divided into teams and began playing games.

If I had tried this same exercise with my girls' volleyball camp, it would have been a miserable failure. After the second whistle, one of the 12-year-olds would have said, "This is dumb. What do you want us to do, stand up or sit down? We'll be glad to do whichever you ask, and just tell us, you don't need that whistle."

Regarding power, males ask three simple questions:

- Who has the whistle?

- How do I get the whistle?

- How do I keep the whistle?

Most decide that once you get the whistle, the best way to keep it is to use it as often as possible.

Females, on the other hand, ask very different questions:

- Do we really need someone with a whistle?

- Is the person with the whistle using it appropriately?

- Is having the whistle really worth the price you pay to get it and keep it?

Most decide they will train for whistle-blowing positions, but once in them, they will use the whistle very sparingly, if at all, thereby proving that whistles are not really necessary.

Clueless

I spent most of my life and early career in groups of women. I participated in team sports from the ages of 12 through 24, and I coached women's volleyball for the next 13 years. At age 38, I moved from coaching into administration. My new role in our department was fundraising and personnel management. My world changed dramatically. I moved from the leader of a group of women to an underling in a group of men.

When I was promoted to a position as associate athletics director, I was the junior player on a three-person management team. The boss was the director of athletics—a sixty-something white male who had been a high-profile men's basketball coach. The second in command was another associate athletics director—a fifty-something white male who had made a career in athletics administration. I rounded out the troika—a late thirties, white, female, former volleyball coach. This was a new situation for all of us—for me, it was my first experience working daily with men; for them, it was their first experience working daily with a woman who was not a secretary.

The other associate and I were both loyal, hardworking, and deeply committed to our boss, but that was the end of our similarities. He was reserved and careful with his feedback, and intensely private in his dealings with others. I was outspoken and gregarious. If he did not have a strong opinion on an issue, he kept silent. I had an opinion on everything and gave it whether it was asked for or not. Most of the time he agreed with the AD. I did not hesitate to disagree or to tell him what he did not want to hear.

I thought of our group meetings as forums to share problems and frustrations; he thought of them as places to share information in a concise, need-to-know fashion. He was very conscious of hierarchy; I was relatively oblivious to it, especially early in my new role. He saw his job as handling problems and difficult issues before they got to the boss; I saw mine as bringing them to him for discussion with a preferred solution in tow. Clearly, I was more verbal and extroverted, but our personality differences were magnified by our divergent gender predilections.

My view of the world influenced my style of interaction. I had just left a world of consensus decision-making, relationship-based exchanges, and relatively flat structural systems. I was comfortable and confident inside this worldview and had made the typical mistake of assuming the rest of the world shared it.

My counterpart had worked for years in a system characterized by top-down decision-making, efficacy-based exchanges, and limited feedback loops. He reflexively filled his role in this structure. He knew when to speak and when to remain silent based on tacit parameters that had become second nature to him in his years in the system.

Fortunately, we admired and respected each other, and genuinely enjoyed each other's company and humor. Consequently, our differences in personality and perspective did not affect our ability to work together.

The President's Decision

When we were in the closing stages of selecting a new football coach, the athletics director scheduled a Sunday in late November for final interviews. We had done the initial screening and interviewing off campus and scheduled these final conversations away from campus also. The plan was to charter a plane, take the president and other key decision-makers, and interview the candidates at a site near their homes. The travel party consisted of the president, the athletics director, the senior associate, and an assistant with twenty years of football experience.

I really wanted to go and was pleased when the AD invited me into his office and told me he thought it would be good experience for me. I thanked him for including me. He said, "No problem, but you need to understand the nature of this process … I mean, it's the president's decision." I shook my head vigorously to indicate I understood. The AD continued in an almost paternal tone, "This is his chance to ask questions and evaluate, you know …" Again, I bobbed my head. "I mean, this will be good for you to go, but …" He obviously wanted to tell me something, but was struggling to find the right words.

I said, "Don't worry, I won't talk too much." He relaxed and laughed, saying, "I want you to participate, just … just …" "Just know when to shut up," I finished for him. He nodded appreciatively.

I had worked for him for three years and he knew I was not as attuned to structural hierarchy and ritual as most men. He also knew other people on the trip would not be as understanding of my unconscious disregard for status or my penchant for participation.

The Fine Art of Negotiating

For 22 years, our institution had played its men's basketball games in a large downtown arena. The city built the facility with the understanding that the University would play its home games there. As the years went by, we became increasingly convinced that the lease arrangement favored the city, to the detriment of our athletics department. The chief negotiator for the city was an irascible character who threw down take-it-or-leave-it terms that made us feel and look powerless. No other playing facilities in the community would be able to accommodate our season-ticket base, so we were at a serious disadvantage when renegotiating more favorable terms.

The athletics director and men's basketball coach, who were both wildly popular, convinced the president that we should investigate the idea of building a new arena on campus. The coach said brashly that the money could be raised in two weeks. He complained about access to the downtown arena for practice and bemoaned the arrival of a minor league hockey team.

No one thought the city could support two large arenas, and it became clear immediately that the downtown area had no options for paying its bills without the University's basketball team as a tenant. Public officials and the Chamber of Commerce urged a more palatable lease agreement for the University. The mayor offered to remove the downtown arena board chairman if necessary. The arena board approved funds for a feasibility study to upgrade their facility. Local business leaders promised a "whatever it takes" approach to keep the basketball team at the downtown site.

This was exactly what we wanted—leverage to sit at the negotiating table as partners. Our president, however, seemed suddenly taken with the idea of an on-campus facility. Even when initial investigations revealed that the building could cost one hundred million dollars, he wanted to pursue the project. The idea of paying debt and operating costs on that costly of a facility was mind-boggling to us in the athletics department and seemed to make no sense from a town/gown perspective either. But the president held firm, saying he wanted an extensive feasibility study, and at each meeting he seemed more and more enthusiastic about the new building.

As time dragged on and no decision was made, public officials, business leaders, university faculty, and the media started to panic a bit. No one but a few diehard basketball fans and those looking to upgrade their seats thought a new arena was a good idea, and even they had no idea how expensive it would be. The meetings about the facility became more secretive and took on a backroom air. Documents were exchanged in draft form to protect them from sunshine laws; only one copy of proposals was delivered to the campus and locked in the president's office; and fewer and fewer people were invited to participate in updates on the process.

The athletics director became very frustrated with the situation. Privately, he told us he would resign if the president made the decision to build the new building. He knew a new arena would saddle us with massive debt, would stick the city with a tax-draining white elephant downtown, and would ruin the president's reputation with his faculty. Further, he thought the delays were hurting our negotiating position with the city and fostering unnecessary ill will between the University and the community.

As strongly as he felt privately, publicly and in face-to-face situations he supported the president completely. At the president's behest, he feigned anger in a meeting with city officials. He argued with an increasingly jittery citizenry that the University had a responsibility to fully investigate all options. He defended the lumbering process to a hostile media, and he shielded the president where he could from the wrath of the faculty.

From our conversations, I could sense he thought he was entangled in a high stakes loyalty test. The president was his boss and he never questioned that it was his role to support him. As much as he hoped the president recognized the illogic of a new arena, the athletics director also knew that he needed to keep his mouth shut and support the president's management of the process.

It was a great lesson for me. I admired the athletics director for his strong, principled leadership style, yet in this situation I saw him suppress his own agenda to play a supportive role. His threat to resign, I realized, was a symptom of his frustration shared only with close confidants and never given as an ultimatum to the president.

Once the feasibility study for the on-campus arena was finished, the downtown group virtually raced to the negotiating table. They offered a long-term lease that was very favorable to the University and promised upgrades to the facility at city expense. The president did lose significant political capital with the faculty and he became a favorite target of the local newspaper, but he solidified his reputation as a ballsy negotiator. He seemed completely indifferent to his lack of popularity and singularly proud of closing such a tough deal.

Leadership

Many conundrums surround women in leadership positions. How and when to assert power? What messages are conveyed by attention to the traditional trappings of status? When can these be ignored? When is ignoring them inadvisable? Certainly, males in leadership must deal with these issues too, but the ready availability of models makes their choices more straightforward. Most women have realized that wholesale mimicry of the male model will not work for them, but where and how to tweak it is still an individual adventure.

Comfort Levels

In the spring of 1996, the University of Tennessee won the NCAA Women's Basketball National Championship. A senior point guard named Michelle Marciniak was instrumental in their victory. In the post-game interview on national television, Michelle's first statement was, "I'm so happy for Pat. We've all worked hard for this, but Pat deserves this championship more than anyone." She was referring to the head coach of the Tennessee team, Pat Head Summitt. She used her head coach's first name in a casual, unself-conscious way, indicating it was their standard form of address.

The remark struck me. I had spent the previous three years working primarily around male athletic teams. The only time male athletes used a coach's first name was in private settings among friends as a smart-aleck form of disrespect. Even though I had coached women's volleyball for 13 years, I had forgotten the comfortable familiarity that characterized functional female groups.

On the Tennessee women's basketball team, no question of leadership existed—everyone knew who was in charge—yet by dispensing with surname formality, Coach Summitt had strengthened the attachment between herself and her team. Since feeling interdependently linked precedes optimal performance for most females, encouraging connectivity is critical.

I stumbled onto this insight myself in a conversation with one of my assistants. I mentioned previously in this chapter my trepidation about asking my female subordinates to make lunch runs. One day, I was in a bind—the boss had told me to join him on a conference call in his office and to send out for lunch. None of my fall-back options was available.

I took twenty dollars to my assistant and said, "I know this isn't part of your job description, but could I impose on you to go get us a couple of sandwiches?" She readily acquiesced, saying, "Sure, I don't mind at all." Feeling guilty, I said, "I promise I won't make this a habit, I know you're not my personal errand runner, and I do truly appreciate it." She raised a hand to silence me and said, "I'm not doing this because you're my boss, I'm doing this because you're my friend."

The message in her words was that our relationship was the factor that made my request acceptable, not our respective positions in the organizational chart. The fact that we shared more than just an office and organizational goals made it easier for her to work for me. Camaraderie does not guarantee optimal performance in women, but it is a more powerful motivator than traditional incentives.

Disregard for structural convention is just one of the characteristics that separates female leadership styles from male. In fact, the difficulties around leadership development are the opposite for women and men. Women often avoid head-to-head confrontation and negatively sanction each other for overt acts of assertiveness. Male groups reward aggression and are characterized by constant struggles for supremacy. Women will flatten workplace hierarchies and ignore traditional symbols of power in the interest of strengthening relationships and promoting camaraderie. Males will create symbols of rank and a pecking order of duties so it is clear to all who has authority.

Office size and location, company car size, private restroom facilities, seating location at events, and club memberships are all emblematic of power and status. They are visual representations of authority, and, from the male perspective, necessary and deserved perquisites.

The female tendency, stemming from our worldview of community, is to belittle the importance of these status symbols. I found myself doing this when I moved into a new position of leadership in our department. I prided myself in the fact that I continued to drive a mid-size car as opposed to the luxury models of my male counterparts; I refused to use the private parking place that was reserved for me outside our office building.

When I traveled with various teams, I was uncomfortable with the habit of those at my rank of moving straight from the plane to the bus and leaving others to unload the luggage. I usually trailed to the back of the plane and assisted with the loading and unloading. These minor displays of ordinariness were more comfortable to me than the alternatives and served to connect me with those I was hired to manage.

I saw this "leveling of the playing field" tendency among my female colleagues also. Several years ago, a woman athletics director at a school in our conference hired a male to coach her women's basketball team. To provide a better working environment for the new staff, she traded her office suite for the former basketball offices, which were considerably smaller. She explained to me that the inconvenience was minimal for her and that she felt this was an important sign of her commitment to the basketball program. From conversations with her coaches, I know they think of her as a caring and capable administrator who is very interested in serving their needs.

Although an important strength of the female leadership style, camaraderie with colleagues and subordinates is only part of the equation for success. We fool ourselves if we ignore both the real and symbolic linkages between power and leadership.

Sometimes *Where* You Are Is All That Matters

We were in the process of building a new academic center for our student-athletes. I toured the construction site regularly with donors who had contributed to the project. I was struck by the small size of the office we had designated for our director of student-athlete services. She was second-in-command in that sector and the space allocation did not reflect her rank.

I called her to my office one morning and mentioned it to her. She said that the office was not optimal, but that she really wanted to be downstairs in the new center where she could be more hands-on with students and accessible to the employees she supervised. She had been designated a larger office on the second floor in the original plans, but had requested the change.

There was a good-sized project room next to the space that had been designated for her office. I suggested she lobby to have the functions switched. She said office size was "really no big deal" to her, and that she felt uncomfortable asking for a larger space. I said square footage might be no big deal to her, but that in the world of work, office size is a symbol of status. She acquiesced after I convinced her that the silent message of a larger office would benefit her in doing her job.

Conscious as I was of these hidden messages, I also needed reminders about symbols of status. A woman who is one of our major donors and had also become a good friend advised me on what I was missing. She was a successful businesswoman in her early sixties who owned several small companies. As a diehard sports fan, she followed our men's basketball team to as many post-season events as she could fit into her work schedule.

In the 1998 NCAA Men's Basketball Tournament, our team pulled a thrilling come-from-behind victory over a favored Duke team. The game was a regional final, played in St. Petersburg, Florida. The victory earned our team a trip to the Final Four and was vindication for a Duke defeat we had suffered several years earlier. Our team had been behind by as many as 17 points well into the second half of the game but had managed to claw back for a four-point win.

After the final horn sounded, bedlam broke out in the Kentucky section and on the floor. I had made my way down to the bench area late in the game and used my official pass to get onto the floor. I joined in the celebration immediately after the game, congratulating the players and coaches. I purposefully stayed to the side of the court, thinking that center stage belonged to the participants, not the administrators.

I was relieved when our ticket manager approached me and asked if I would help her get our Final Four tickets from the regional host and carry them to the bus. She also enlisted the help of a young man who worked for us intermittently, warning both of us that the bags were very heavy and needed to be carried quite a distance. I preferred the opportunity to be useful to staying on the floor so I scurried off with her to claim our treasures.

A week later, I was at the Final Four walking back from a president's brunch with my donor friend. She said to me, "You know, if you really want to succeed, you need to be more visible." I asked her what she meant. She said, "Well, where were you after the Duke game? The other administrators were on the floor celebrating with the team." I explained that I had gone with our ticket manager to pick up our Final Four tickets and carry them to the bus. She said, "That's what I mean. At your level and position, you need to be on the floor; get someone else to schlep tickets." I explained my feelings that the celebration should be for the players and coaches, not the rest of us, and that I had jumped at the opportunity to provide a needed service to our ticket manager.

She said, "I understand how you feel, I'm just telling you as a friend and someone who has played this game a long time, there are times when you need to exercise your rank. People need to see you on the floor after a game like that mingling with the president, the coaches, and others." I continued to protest, saying I thought that was so phony, such grandstanding, and such an obvious attention-seeking ploy.

In her gentle manner, as only a friend could, she said, "Listen, sometimes to get ahead you have to act like a shit, but believe me, it's an important part of the game, and, I can tell you from experience, after awhile you get used to it." We both laughed loudly.

After we won the national championship a day later, I stayed on the floor in a visible spot until the final snip of the last net.

A February 17, 1997, *TIME* magazine article discusses the issue of women and power in a political context. The article documents Madeleine Albright's life and career, culminating with her appointment as the first female Secretary of State. Author Nancy Gibbs points out: "Albright knew early on that you can't do a thing in foreign policy without power." She made her status obvious by renaming the Monday briefings from BAC (Berger, Albright, Cohen) to ABC (Albright, Berger, Cohen). She made sure her appointees knew they were obligated to her, not the President, for their position. She let people know that her management style was to disregard bureaucratic structure, and told a powerful group to "get used to it." Gibbs concludes that, "Even her [Albright's] closest friends are not sure how she plans to wield her power. But any student of Munich—and any legatee of the Holocaust—must have absorbed this lesson of power: that failing to use it can be just as dangerous as using it unwisely." (15)

I doubt that these observations about the use of power would have been made in an article about a male Secretary of State. Albright's gender made the issues worth mentioning. Gibbs tacitly and correctly assumes that a woman's ability to negotiate the map-less labyrinth surrounding her use of power will determine her success or failure in a heretofore all-male hierarchy.

Most women are skittish about utilizing power. We perceive the exercise of power as a separation of people into "us" and "them," and as visible symbols of one-upmanship. These are the very characteristics that make power work in a hierarchical system; these characteristics separate the leaders from the followers.

Pat Heim notes that women view exercising power as dangerous. She tries to allay our fears by defining power as "the ability to get things done," yet she concedes that "while it's comfortable and easy for a man to be both powerful and masculine, it's much more difficult for a woman to pull off being powerful and feminine." (18)

I was involved in a meeting with our men's basketball coach and athletics director to resolve a dispute over practice time in the gym we shared. I argued vigorously on behalf of my program. At one point, I became incensed and told the coach that what he was complaining about was "bullshit." The next day, the athletics director came into my office grinning from ear to ear. The coach had told him, "I like DeBoer, she's got balls." Our dispute was resolved to our mutual satisfaction.

His compliment was backhanded at best, and serves to focus on the conundrum identified by Heim and facing women in leadership positions—either be identified with maleness or risk being identified with ineptness. Avoidance of the exercise of power, our socialized tendency, will bring questions, particularly from male staffers and colleagues, about our willingness and ability to lead. On the other hand, the conventional exercise of power will ostracize female staffers and colleagues, who will view these acts as unnecessary dividers. To succeed, women leaders must be androgynous hybrids of these two tendencies—picking our battles very carefully, yet aggressively engaging once the fight begins.

Conclusion

Many of today's workplaces are still hierarchically structured. The organizational chart is triangular in shape. The lines of authority are clearly defined.

Paul Saffo, director of the Institute for the Future, a 30-year-old trend-forecasting organization, made these comments about organizational structure in a 1996 interview: "For the past 100 years, US companies have been built on a now-fraying hierarchical management structure. In the coming decade, look for this model to continue to erode, probably to the point of wholesale abandonment ... . Company organizations will be web-like. Rigid hierarchies will dissolve in favor of rich, flexible, and constantly changing relationship webs. Power will be determined less by title than by one's position in the web." (17)

He attributes this change to the rapid development of information technologies and the subsequent necessary empowerment of employees within all levels of an organization. He never references gender in his interview, nor does he attribute any of his predicted changes to an increase in the number of women in workplace structures.

Our use of the same words caught my eye. We had independently chosen identical imagery to describe two different things. I used the images of hierarchy and web to describe divergent gender cultures; he used these same images to describe past and future workplace cultures.

Management guru Tom Peters agrees with Saffo's assessment of future workplace structures. In a 1991 taped presentation entitled "LIVE," he goes beyond Saffo and makes the link to gender. He says, "… In a world where companies cease to be companies and become networks of companies, then managing networks and relationships becomes the single most significant task of the institution: which is why by the year 2005 there won't be many jobs available in this country for men. John Wayne's days are numbered … . [T]he ability to indeed manage networks, which tends to be a skill which women are a little bit better at to hugely better at than men is a very important part of that process." (18)

Obviously, Peter's message is full of hyperbole, but his point and Saffo's are the same: where organizations of the past favored traditional male managerial skills, organizations of the future will likely value historically female managerial talents. For several decades, women like me have benefited from studying and, at times, mimicking male behavior. Now men, challenged by changing workplace cultures and the need to adapt their style to be effective, can benefit from studying and, when appropriate, mimicking female managerial styles.

Solutions

In 1973, 11% of Fortune 1000 companies had women on their boards. By 1993, the number had changed to more than 50%. (1) In 1999, for the first time, women outnumbered men in American colleges and universities. (2) Women receive over half of all master's degrees and one-third of all doctorates. (3)

These statistics tell only part of the story about men and women at work. The environment is growing increasingly competitive. In 1987, one worker in twenty (5%) was promoted to top management. Due to advances in technology, corporate downsizing, and the aging of the baby boomers, by 2001, that number was down to one in fifty (2%). (4)

Employability and promotability in the workplace will always depend on proper education, requisite skills, and appropriate experience. However, in any job requiring supervision, the abilities to communicate, direct, and lead are paramount.

Our different gender cultures impact communication in both cross-gender and same-gender situations. Since gender-integrated workplaces are increasingly the norm and downsized efficiency looks to be the permanent standard in this country, men and women have little choice but to learn to work side by side.

Understanding the other's paradigm is a start. Seamlessly switching between cultures is the major challenge. A competitive advantage is the reward.

Rambling vs. Cutting to the Chase

As I was writing this book, I asked a male friend to read the early chapters. He said he enjoyed my anecdotes and thought I had relevant ideas about gender, but he wanted to know what was the point of my writing. He asked if there would be any chapters dealing with how to solve the problems created by gender differences. My husband had the same response to my initial drafts. They both wanted to know: When was I going to get to the solutions portion of my manual?

I found their feedback enlightening. I said I intended that my analysis provide the tools for individual problem solving; I contended that building awareness and empathy to differences should be sufficient to cause change in behavior. They disagreed, saying awareness was necessary, but not sufficient. My book needed directions for specific action.

As I pondered their thoughts, I was struck that we were playing out a typical gender difference in communication. My male advisors were frustrated by my extensive detailing of the problem, and were eager for solutions. They wanted me to get to the point, which, for them, were concrete directions that would produce measurable results.

On the other hand, I was much more concerned with being understood. I doubted my authority to give behavioral instructions to others. I knew I would resent being spoon-fed instructions on how to respond to newfound awareness. When reading self-help books, I always read the theory and skip the exercises. My male advisors said they never read these kinds of books because they contained too much whining about problems and not enough pragmatic advice.

In deference to their advice and to assist those seeking concrete directions, in this chapter, I have highlighted specific do's and don'ts for cross-gender communication in the workplace, and used anecdotes to explain them. The first set of instructions is based on this exchange with these two men.

For Women

When bringing an issue or problem to a male colleague, get to the point; tell him what the issue or problem is and stop talking. Resist the temptation to explain the details surrounding the problem unless you are asked for more information. Providing peripheral information to males is perceived as rambling and time-wasting.

For Men

When bringing an issue or problem to a female colleague, explain the details; tell her why you are bringing her the issue, why you think it is a problem, and what are peripheral concerns. Force yourself to provide all the information that might be relevant. Failure to do so is perceived as a lack of perceptiveness about the nuances of a situation.

"What Do You Think?"

When Rick Pitino left the University of Kentucky to take the job as basketball coach and general manager of the Boston Celtics, it left us with a vacancy in our most high-profile position. The media interest in our choice for the next coach was intense. Reporters camped out near our offices and stalked our every move. Each day's news was full of speculation and opinions. As we had previously faced the possibility of Pitino's departure, we had had numerous internal discussions about possible replacements.

C.M. Newton, our athletics director, wanted to move quickly if he could. He got the president's approval to do some informal investigating. He called the senior associate and me into a meeting the afternoon of the press conference announcing Pitino's departure. He opened the meeting by saying, "I really want to hire Tubby Smith for this job. He worked here for a couple of years, so I have confidence that he knows how tough this job is. What do you think?" I looked at the senior associate. He said, "I think it's a good idea. Let's do it."

I agreed that Tubby Smith was a good first choice for us. My natural tendency, however, would have been to raise some fundamental issues for discussion. I wanted us to verbally dissect all the pros and cons of this option, to turn it upside down and inside out, to ensure we had considered every possible consequence of the decision. Sensing conversation was inappropriate, I suppressed my instinct and said simply, "Sounds like the best plan to me." Both men seemed comfortable with our limited exchange.

I left the meeting unsure that I had fulfilled my role as support staff. I realize now that that situation—"What do you think?"—did not really mean, "What do you think?" This was a time to play by the strict rules of hierarchy. The leader had made a decision and the appropriate response was affirmation.

I contrast that situation with an exchange I had with an assistant when I was the head volleyball coach at Kentucky. We had had several informal discussions about the tactics we were using in our defensive system. In our final meeting before beginning training, I raised the issue for debate. I said, "I'm leaning toward a modified middle-back deep system. I think this suits our personnel best, especially with the experience we have at the middle-back position. What do you think?" She said, "Good idea. Let's do it."

Her response irritated me. I expected discussion. I wanted her to voice her concerns, to debate the pros and cons of my suggestion, to enlighten me on aspects of my plan that I had not considered. I wanted to know she had given it as much thought as I had. I wanted her to be a partner in making this critical decision. Her ready acquiescence made me feel cheated. I did not think she was taking ownership in the decision and this worried me. I did not value affirmation as much as I did argument. "What do you think?" really meant, "What do you think?"

The hierarchical perspective is that opinions are valued and weighted based on the position of the opinion-holder. If the leader expresses a strong opinion, those mindful of the structure will frequently agree, realizing their personal opinions are neither sought nor relevant. This willingness to accept a subordinate role and recognition of another's status is considered good team play.

The web culture holds that all opinions have value and may be instructive in a debate. The role of others is to enlighten and inform the decision-maker of perspectives they may not have considered and, if they feel the decision-maker has erred, to question and express disagreement. This willingness to do one's part and concern for the well-being of the group and/or organization is considered good team play.

For Women

When working in a hierarchical structure, be cautious with expressing opinions if you are an underling in the structure. Those in charge may interpret questioning and disagreement as either insubordination or simple cluelessness. Even when you are asked, assess whether dissenting feedback is appropriate. If the decision-maker has already decided, the request is more likely an opportunity to affirm their viewpoint than an invitation for input.

For Men

When working in a flat structure, realize that input is not only welcome but also expected. Volunteer non-judgmental feedback. Those without opinions are perceived as ambivalent and uninterested. Be prepared to courteously express your viewpoint, particularly if you are asked. The request is an indicator that your perspective is valued even if it contradicts that of the boss. Ready acquiescence may be viewed as a renunciation of your responsibility to the management team.

Executive Women's Golf (EWG) and Professional Men's Shopping (PMS)

Several years ago, I attended a mixer hosted by a group called Executive Women's Golf (EWG). The goal of the organization as stated in their brochure was, "To teach managerial women how to play golf in a non-threatening environment. Learn the rules of the game, basic swing mechanics, and golf etiquette in fun and competition-free surroundings." The evening's recruitment event included a cocktail hour, dinner, and a brief presentation by the president.

During the cocktail hour, I joined a group of three women visiting in a circle and listened to their conversation: "Hi, I'm Sharon," said a short stout woman, extending her hand, "how are you?" Before anyone could answer, she volunteered, "I really don't even know why I came tonight. I'm the world's worst golfer." "Oh, that can't be," all three of us chimed in simultaneously. "No, really," persisted Sharon. "The first time out, I drove the cart right onto the place where you hit from—what do they call it—some kind of box. Anyway, right then and there, my husband said he would never play with me again."

"Sharon, don't fret," said a slender blond. "I'm Sally, our kids are both at Morton Middle School; I've seen you there picking yours up. Anyway, you cannot be as bad a golfer as I am. Most of the time, I have to swing three or four times before I even hit the ball and then who knows where it will go." All of us nodded empathetically.

"No, no girls, neither of you can top this," inserted a pretty brunette. "Listen to this: I head out to my first corporate golf outing last week. My husband goes to them all the time and says it's a great way to make contacts. Well, he has this old set of clubs and he gives me a bunch of balls. I bought this cute little outfit that doesn't make me look as fat as I am," at which point the rest of us gasp collectively, saying, "You're not fat." She continues without acknowledging our remark, "Anyway, I'm thinking this is supposed to be fun, right, just a bunch of folks spending an afternoon in the sun getting to know each other and making sales. Well, my husband tells me, 'Honey, I don't have any gloves that will fit you, so buy a couple when you get to the clubhouse. Just put them on my account.'

"So, of course, I'm late getting there and everyone is loaded on their carts as I drive up. I hate things that start on time, don't you?" Again she continues before we can reply, "I let a nice young man take my clubs and I fly into the clubhouse for some gloves. Well, they are so expensive! $16 … so I just get one set; I mean $16—you can buy a decent pair of leather gloves for that! I run out and jump in the cart with a guy named Sam who seemed nice at the time—but was smoking one of those smelly cigars. Yuk, but I figured you couldn't play a sporting event and smoke so he would be putting it out shortly. Anyway, we get to the first place to hit and I unpack my new gloves and wouldn't you know it, they shorted me one. I only had one left-handed glove in the package. Well, by now I'm mad. I did all this rushing around, paid way too much for these gloves anyway, am gagging and starting to smell like a dirty cigar, and now only one glove. I say, 'I can't believe it, they shorted me a glove.' Sam, the guy who was supposed to be nice, rolls his eyes and says, 'This is gonna be a long day.'

"Well, I try to ignore his remark; I mean he doesn't even know me well enough to be sarcastic like that, but I'm still mad about the glove, so I say, 'Listen, why don't you fellows start. They shorted me a glove at the clubhouse and I'm going to run back there and get a pair.' They all look at me like I'm crazy. One guy says, 'Don't you want to take a cart? We're a ways out here.' Well of course I didn't, I mean this is supposed to be a sporting event, right. I just ran on back to the clubhouse, telling every group that I passed that I had been shorted a glove at the pro shop, flapping my one glove to prove it. *Every group!*"

"OK, so maybe you girls already know this, but I didn't: They sell golf gloves as ones! How embarrassed am I? The nice boy in the pro shop said he would drive me back out to my group but the thought of passing all those people who knew that I didn't know you bought golf gloves in ones was a little too much. I held back until I got to my car and then I bawled all the way home. Anyway, one of the men at the pro shop gave me the brochure about this event and said I should definitely come. So I'm here, but I don't know if I'm going to like this game."

I wandered from one group to another during the social hour. The conversations were similar in nature, subject matter, and tone—each woman describing herself as a terrible golfer. In fact, they competed to be "the most terrible." They took turns telling of a humiliating moment or an embarrassing score. They stood in tight circles of three or four, often touching each other's hands or arms during a poignant moment in the story. They looked at each other's faces and laughed often at themselves and each other. The storytelling and laughter continued through dinner with tales of naive mistakes and humbling faux pas.

After dinner, the president spoke for about fifteen minutes. She began by trying to convince all the women in the room that they could not possibly be a worse golfer than she was. Then she made a soft-sell pitch for EWG, telling us the intent was to learn golf in a non-competitive, non-threatening atmosphere, that it didn't cost very much to join the organization, and that no level of ineptitude would disqualify us.

Let's imagine a male counterpart to this group. Men realize that women hold most positions of power at work and that they must find ways to be invited to their activities, and to be present when and where the deals are cut. They form an organization, called Professional Men's Shopping (PMS), a male-only support group designed to teach men the basics of shopping.

The brochure for the organization, targeted at men, gives the following sales pitch: "Learn to shop with the Big Girls. See the latest equipment and hear advice from a pro. Improve your shopping efficiency by 50% in one evening or get your money back, guaranteed!"

Listen to the cocktail conversation from this gathering:

"Hey, I'm John Alexander from Toyota. You know this shopping stuff is not nearly as tough as I thought. I went out Saturday for the first time and did three hours, didn't feel a thing."

"Three hours?" responds a man standing next to John. "Not bad for the JV team. I'm Bob Smith, senior vice president at Lexmark. I did the biggest mall in town for five hours straight, no break. Now that's some shopping." Seeing a cocktail waitress, he barks, "Honey, over here, grab me another Budweiser?"

"Pah! You clowns don't even get it," says another man standing in the same lineup. "I'm telling you, it has nothing to do with how much time you spend, it's how many stores you hit." Pointing both his thumbs at his chest, he says proudly, "Two hundred and fifty-six stores in one day, try that on for size."

The men gather in amoeba-like groups that are fluid, with little form or cohesion. Most of the time, they do not face each other but stand at wide angles, each looking elsewhere around the room. They shake hands when introducing themselves but otherwise do not touch each other. Their talk is loud, boisterous, and exclamatory. They exchange information, recite facts, and trade innocent barbs.

The president of PMS opens his speech with a couple of off-color jokes. Then, he tells the audience that he left a very lucrative position to join PMS because he saw unlimited potential in the organization. His appeal focuses heavily on the networking benefits of becoming an elite shopper. He discounts the myths that shopping is just idle time-wasting and that bargain hunting is for sissies. He brags about the money, position, and power he has gained since learning to shop.

The interactions in the respective groups are typical. Conversation has a very different function in male and female groups, particularly among strangers. Women share vulnerabilities and hide strengths when with strangers to make others feel comfortable and accepted. Men share strengths and hide vulnerabilities in the same circumstance to establish rank and set boundaries. Women face each other; men stand side by side. Women praise each other and mock themselves. Men praise themselves and mock each other. For women, the getting-to-know-you small talk of casual conversation is a means to connection; for men, this same talk is a means to differentiate.

For Women

When talking to men, realize that, for them, conversations are not exchanges designed to promote closeness or understanding. If you share a mistake or vulnerability as an invitation to openness, do not expect him to reciprocate. He will be baffled that you are sharing a weakness with a stranger and he will likely subconsciously brand you as someone lacking self-confidence and savvy.

For Men

When talking to women, realize for them, conversations are not about maintaining or establishing status. If you share an accomplishment or voice a criticism in the interests of establishing your rank or displaying your knowledge, do not expect her to reciprocate by competing or disagreeing with you. As opposed to the invitation to spar you had intended, she will likely brand you a know-it-all lacking self-confidence and poise.

Why Talk About It?

I work with a young man in his thirties whose wife works in a daycare center. He has shared with me repeatedly that his wife comes home after work and complains endlessly about her job and her coworkers. He says when he gets home, he wants to forget about work. Even when he has had a bad day, he figures complaining to his wife will change nothing, and could cause her to worry needlessly.

Her habit irritated him so much that finally he told her he was unwilling to listen to her whining. She could do something to fix her problems (and he had already given her several solutions), she could quit, or she could complain to someone else. Now, he reports, she comes home, calls a female friend who works with her, and they talk on the phone for an hour about the work situation they just left. He finds this behavior unproductive, depressing, and futile.

My colleague's story, although personal in nature, is indicative of another common gender difference in communication. Females tend to solve problems, or at least feel better about dealing with them, by discussing them. Verbalizing difficulties, dissecting interactions, and sharing hardships are ways that women connect with others. This interaction eases our distress about difficulties and enhances our confidence in our ability to manage them. Talk is the fiber that links those in the web. It builds the fellowship that makes women feel comfortable and self-assured.

Males tend to solve problems, or at least feel better about dealing with them, by ignoring or suppressing them. They silently ponder a problem until a solution comes to them. Talking about problems before you fully understand them or without solutions in mind may lead others to think you cannot handle them. The life habit of hiding vulnerabilities rules their psyche and makes disclosure of difficulties synonymous with admitting you are a failure.

For women, then, problems are dissipated by talk; for men, they are exaggerated by talk. Women become more self-confident through agenda-less conversation about difficulties. Men become more self-confident by silently coping with hardship. Each gender finds the other's habit baffling and dysfunctional.

John Gray, in his book *Men are from Mars, Women are from Venus*, spends a whole chapter discussing these differences in problem-solving styles. He says:

> "One of the biggest differences between men and women is how they cope with stress. Men become increasingly focused and withdrawn, while women become increasingly overwhelmed and emotionally involved. At these times, a man's needs for feeling good are different from a woman's. He feels better by solving problems, while she feels better by talking about problems. Not understanding and accepting these differences creates unnecessary friction in our relationships." (5)

Gray's book is written for men and women in intimate relationships. However, his message is transferable to workplace exchanges. Men must understand that women *talk* their way through problems. Women must understand that men *work* their way through problems. Conversation is the healing balm for women that solitariness is for men.

For Women

Share your re-occurring problems with other women or trustworthy workplace colleagues with lower rank and status. Men will perceive your talk as whining and will view you as less competent and self-assured.

The opposite of too much talk is too little. Men working for or with women may suffer unanticipated consequences because of their gender-related habit of non-disclosure. Women expect communication.

My best friend is an attorney who works as the director of a Friend of the Court office. The role of her office is to represent the interests of children of divorcing parents by setting, collecting, and monitoring child-support payments. She has two male employees and 14 female employees in her office. The work is emotionally draining, especially for the supervisors and support investigators. Her staff is close, as they spend a lot of time talking through cases and issues, identifying and fighting their own biases, and providing support and reinforcement to each other.

The assistant director is male. He solves problems independently and rarely seeks or gives feedback. He responds to input with a blank stare and, at most, a slight nod of his head. This habit really irritates his female coworkers. They perceive him as uncommunicative, uncaring, and inept. My friend—his boss—says he is a hard worker, a capable attorney, and sensitive to the issues in their workplace. However, his failure to interact has hurt his credibility and perceived competence among his female colleagues.

For Men

Talk to female colleagues and superiors. They expect it and perceive withdrawal as dysfunctional behavior. Unwillingness to discuss problems and to give and receive feedback is interpreted by women as a lack of self-awareness and maturity.

Men cannot understand women until they grasp the female-defining nature of expressing oneself. Women cannot understand men until they grasp the male-defining nature of proving oneself. The result of one is talk; the result of the other is silence.

Do You Think We Can Sell the House?

My 13 years of collegiate coaching were punctuated by several stunning victories and a few agonizing defeats. These matches, only a handful of the 400-or-so I coached, are etched in my memory in great detail because of the significance that they had for me and my program. One of the most memorable losses occurred late in my career and haunts me mostly because of the unusual depth of my anguish over the defeat.

We were playing a team from one of the smaller state universities that had pleaded with us for a spot on our schedule. They had never beaten us in the twenty years that each of our schools had sponsored volleyball programs. It was late in our season and the match fell on a Wednesday night. The crowd was paltry and uninterested, as the opponent was not deemed worthy. We prepared poorly, played even worse, and lost the match in four games.

The loss hurt me. I was angry with myself for our lack of preparation, but I knew that was fixable. It was my inability to motivate my team that night and to get them to respond to simple instructions that shook my confidence in a profound way. I felt completely helpless on the sideline. I stayed in my office for an hour after the match looking at the statistics, alternately berating and trying to console myself.

Worn out, I headed for home. My husband was waiting up. He had skipped the match, counting it as an easy and uninteresting win. I slumped into a chair and started sobbing. Between gasps, I lamented that I had lost my effectiveness with my players, that I had way too much administrative work to be a good coach, and that my once-successful program was decaying from the inside out. He listened silently.

A week before, I had shared with him an inquiry from another university regarding my interest in their vacant coaching position. I had nonchalantly turned them away. My program was well-respected and well-established; theirs was struggling and suspect. I ended my self-flagellation by suggesting that I call them back and plead with them to hire me while I still had some credibility left and before I was recognized as a complete, unemployable impostor.

I continued to cry quietly but said no more. After a long pause, he said, "Do you think we can sell the house?"

His focus on a pragmatic detail snapped me out of my lethargy as if I had been slapped in the face. I sniped sarcastically that I had not given a lot of thought to that issue but now that he had brought it up, I would certainly consider it. I got up and walked out of the room.

I wanted empathy. I was feeling overwhelmed and needed reinforcement that I was OK. He took my words literally, hearing what I said instead of what I felt. My melancholy had practical ramifications for him. He heard that I might job hunt and knew that meant relocating. We had just refinanced our house. His plans were that Lexington would be our home for another few years.

Anxiety affected us very differently. My emotional breakdown was a first and necessary step towards recovery from my distress. For me, it was not a pleasant emotion, but certainly not a dangerous one. For him, it was very dangerous. Dealing with anguish through crying was a passive and unproductive response. He panicked, certain I was having a nervous breakdown.

Although this example comes from my personal life, the enlightenment it provided about gender differences helped me deal with similar situations in my work life. I remember a female presenter telling us in a workplace seminar to "die before you cry" when dealing with job stress around males. Her advice stemmed from her observations of male reactions to crying females.

For Women

Avoid sharing a personal crisis with male colleagues and superiors. Your male counterparts probably will not recognize your emotion as a gender-related reaction to stress. They may panic and make value judgments about your emotional stability.

For Men

When confronted with a female colleague who begins to cry, picture her in a rage. She is feeling overwhelmed, and by talking and emoting will regain her composure. Quell your fear of emotion and tendency to respond with rational pragmatism.

My husband's way of dealing with stress was anger. I remember many times in my playing and coaching career when he, as a spectator, would fly into a rage. Generally, my team was playing poorly and the prospect of losing made him feel overwhelmed. He felt helpless to change the course of events. He cared deeply about me and had staked his future on my success.

He would scream at my players, the referees, and me in a booming voice that was intrusive and unmistakable. He derided our efforts, paced the stands like a caged animal, and attacked anyone who questioned his behavior. After the competitions, whether we won or lost, his anger quickly disappeared and his sanity returned.

Rage was his response to feeling overwhelmed. It was the counterpart emotion to my tears. Like my tears, it was not a pleasant emotion for him, but not a dangerous one. For me, it was very dangerous. I had the same reaction to his anger that he had to my tears. I panicked. I read his raging as a personal attack. To me, his fury was an inappropriate and destructive way to respond to distress.

For Women

When confronted with a male colleague who begins to rage, picture him in tears. He is feeling overwhelmed, and by raging and withdrawing will regain his composure. Quell your fear of anger and tendency to take his emotion personally.

For Men

Avoid rage with female colleagues and superiors. Your female counterparts probably will not recognize your anger as a gender-related reaction to stress. They may panic and make value judgments about your emotional stability.

These reactions to stress are obviously gender-related, not gender-specific. Some women rage and some men cry. But generally, women cope with anguish by talking and sometimes by crying. Men cope with anguish by withdrawing and sometimes by raging. Recognizing these patterns in your workplace colleagues will prevent overreaction and misinterpretation of their behavior.

I Feel Your Pain vs. Here's What You Do!

A male coaching friend was telling me of a communication habit of his female boss that really irritated him. He said, "I go to her with a problem, and all I hear is that she has or has had the same problem. That doesn't do me any good."

One of his volleyball players had become pregnant. The player came to him in the fifteenth week of her pregnancy and told him she wanted to have an abortion. His player was extremely distraught and he feared she might do something to hurt herself. She begged him not to tell her parents and to help her.

He examined his alternatives, but was at a loss for an appropriate response. Knowing his decision had ramifications for the university, he sought counsel from his boss. She told him how much she empathized with his dilemma. She related several stories from her own coaching days when she had experienced similar feelings and situations. She talked of all the moral and ethical dilemmas involved. He left her office very frustrated, knowing that his situation was not unique, but not feeling any better equipped to manage it.

He wanted advice. He would never have shared the problem if he thought he could handle it himself. John Gray highlights this gender-related characteristic when he says, "… [A man] rarely talks about his problems unless he needs expert advice… . Asking for help when you can do it yourself is perceived as a sign of weakness … If he truly does need help, … he will find someone he respects and then talk about his problem. Talking about a problem … is an invitation for advice." (6)

My colleague's female boss had responded to his feelings, not his problem. This response was automatic for her. She recognized his feelings of vulnerability and attempted to put him at ease by sharing her own moments of doubt. For women, the first step in problem-solving discussions is to reinforce the other person emotionally. One way to do this is to let the other person know their experience is shared. This puts them at ease and thereby enhances their ability to share their difficulty.

My male colleague took no solace in his female boss' disclosures of similar struggles. In fact, he felt he needed strong guidance, not someone who shared his hesitations about dealing with this problem. In attempting to comfort him by sharing her own confusion and feelings of vulnerability, she had compromised her credibility.

For Women

When a man comes to you with a problem, tell him how to fix it. He expects this and thinks you have expertise. It is the reason he brought the problem to you in the first place. If applicable, you may use an example from your own experience to demonstrate the effectiveness of the solution you propose. But, realize he wants a solution more than he wants empathy.

One of our major contributors who owns several restaurants happened to phone one day when I was struggling with an organizational problem. He innocuously asked how things were going. I lamented that I was frustrated with our system of incentives, and even more frustrated with my inability to convince those above me to change it. I said I thought it was costing us a lot of money.

He immediately launched into an extended discourse on how we could fix our problems. He said we needed to revamp our entire system and gave me the details of how to do it. Then, he told me what to say to my superiors to convince them this was the right way to proceed. Finally, he made several aggressive projections on the new amounts of money we would raise by following his advice.

His arrogance angered me. I thought, "What a pompous know-it-all! This guy doesn't know my job any more than I know the restaurant business. Does he think I'm stupid and haven't already thought of or tried the solutions he is proposing?" I said nothing but ended our conversation quickly. I wanted empathy from him for my feelings of frustration. I wanted to hear that I was not alone in this predicament, that he, too, had experienced moments when he felt boxed in and unable to move in the direction he thought appropriate.

He heard my problem, not my feelings. Since I had confided in him, he figured I must want him to give me a solution. He had no reason to question his expertise in the area. I must have thought he had some or I would not have shared the problem with him in the first place. He accepted the advisor position that I had assigned to him and told me what to do.

For Men

When a woman comes to you with a problem, listen without interrupting her account of the problem. Honestly acknowledge your level of expertise or lack thereof. If applicable, tell of your own uncertainty with a similar situation before suggesting a solution, if you suggest one at all. Realize she wants empathy more than advice.

"Hmm" and "Uh-huh"

James, one of our assistant athletics directors, came into my office one day to update me on a player who had decided to quit our women's track team. Her mother was very upset that we would not grant her daughter a release that would allow her immediate eligibility at another institution. He had had a meeting with the athlete and her mother a week earlier in which he had explained the reasons for our decision. He told me, "I can't believe this dispute is still going on; last week that mother sat in my office and shook her head, smiled, and said 'uh-huh' and 'I see' to everything I said. She made me think she not only understood our position but agreed with it." Then she walked right out the door and carried her protest to the next level.

"Did she ever say she agreed with our position?" I asked him. He thought for a moment, then said, "No, but why would she make me think she agreed?" I answered, "Doesn't sound as if she did. Sounds as if she was just being polite."

Common female habits in conversation are nodding the head, smiling when eye contact is made, and interjecting audible affirmations like "hmm" and "uh-huh." These reinforcements indicate attentiveness; they ease the flow of conversation; they help build and sustain dialog. Most women would say these are simple conversational courtesies.

Males are generally more passive when listening. They may look at the speaker intermittently, but they do not readily nod their heads, smile, or verbally encourage the exchange. Conversation, especially with strangers, is viewed as a means to gather information or state a position. My colleague read the woman's politeness as an unintended affirmation of her agreement.

I notice this difference when speaking to groups. I feel at ease more quickly when presenting to female audiences. Women give me constant feedback that they are listening—they shake their heads, they smile, they meet my eyes, they laugh, they cry. They encourage me to continue.

Male audiences are more reserved. Men evaluate rather than encourage. If I meet their eyes, they either look away or impassively stare back. If they find something funny, they smile instead of laughing. If something touches them, they turn their heads down so no one sees their eyes fill up.

From subsequent feedback, I have come to realize that the differences are gender-related feedback proclivities rather than positive or negative evaluations of my topic or delivery. I realize now that although the reactions are distinct, neither tells me much about either attentiveness to my presentation or acceptance of my point of view.

In her book *Beyond the Double Bind*, Kathleen Hall Jamieson notes these differences in communication styles. She says:

"Women are more likely than men to verbally indicate emotion. This does not mean, however, that women respond to events more emotionally. Instead, it seems that women are more disposed to display their reactions in emotional terms ... . Women look more at the person they are conversing with than men do. Overall, females are more empathic than males; they tend to both give and receive more emotional support than men." (7)

Non-verbal behavior is simply an extension of verbal behavior. Women communicate to bond. Men communicate to convince. The female style encourages exchanges, the male style evaluates exchanges.

For Women

When in conversation with a man, realize that he may mistake politeness for agreement with his statements. If you disagree or do not want to disclose your position, reduce your feedback while he is speaking.

For Men

When in conversation with a woman, do not mistake her engaging demeanor for agreement with your argument. She may be smiling and nodding out of politeness and/or nervousness rather than acquiescence. If you want to encourage conversation and/or feedback, soften your countenance and give her more non-verbal feedback when listening.

Wet-Blanketry vs. Hysteria

In 1994, a donor named Ken pledged a million dollars to our department for the construction of a new softball/soccer complex. I was ecstatic. Our community cared little for these sports, so fundraising for the new complex had been tedious and slow. Ken agreed to pay us $200,000 each January for the next five years. Shortly after making the pledge, he and his wife decided to divorce. The legal proceedings quickly became very contentious. Six months after signing his pledge agreement, his assets were frozen.

Having already committed to programming in both soccer and softball, we started the facility. I had raised some other dollars to support the construction, but Ken's was the major pledge. We needed his money. Each time we talked, he gave effusive assurances that he intended to honor his pledge. When he thought he was nearing the end of the divorce proceedings, he would call and promise to send a check. Then, something would happen to delay the settlement. My colleagues lost confidence in my reports of impending funds and mocked my optimism about Ken's intentions. Finally, in mid-October at an extravaganza we hold annually to celebrate the beginning of the basketball season, he handed me a personal check for $200,000. I was elated and eager for vindication with my brethren. Cavalierly, I put the check in my pocket and plotted a chance to flaunt it in their presence.

Our football team was playing in Baton Rouge the next day. I caught an early morning flight and joined our team at the stadium about two hours before the game. The athletics director had traveled with the football team and was already there. I caught up with him on the sideline of the field. I said, "You're not going to believe what I brought with me." He gave me a sideways glance, rolled his eyes, and said, "What?" I pulled the check out of my wallet and handed it to him. "Huh," he shrugged, "only $800,000 left to go. I hope the rest doesn't take this long to collect. I'm going upstairs to get something to eat. Want to come?"

He may have been relieved that we had started collecting on the pledge, he may have regretted his doubts about the donor, he may have been proud of my work on our behalf. If he felt any of these emotions, he failed to mention them to me. He was not going to show excitement and he definitely was not going to be one-upped by me.

His flippant response had the effect of rain on my parade. I felt deflated. He purposefully declined to share my enthusiasm, not out of malice, but out of habit. His indifference served to remind me that the task was far from complete and that, from his perspective, jubilation was premature.

For Women

When dealing with men, realize they often suppress their emotions. A muted response when you think joy and enthusiasm is appropriate is more likely an indicator of training than true ambivalence. Instead of reading it as wet-blanketry, revel in your gender-related access to full expression.

In May of 1997, we were involved in the final stages of trial preparation for a lawsuit that had been filed against our athletics department 18 months earlier. Testimony from our head coach, who had since left for a pro job, was an important part of our case even though he had been excused from personal liability in the matter. It was the fall of the year, the coach was busy with pre-season with his new team, and the lawsuit had become a low priority for him.

Fortunately, his team was coming to Lexington in mid-October to play an exhibition game. We arranged for the coach to give his testimony on videotape the evening before the game. Protesting loudly about the inconvenience, the plaintiff's attorneys finally agreed to drive the 80 miles from Louisville to Lexington for the evening taping. The team's charter plane was to land at 7:00 p.m. We scheduled the deposition for 7:30 p.m.

We knew our former coach's interests were now miles away from Lexington and that all the issues he would be asked to address had happened several years earlier. I went with two of our attorneys to pick him up at the airport so we could give him a quick refresher course on the case and answer any questions he might have.

At 7:15, the plane was not in radar range. I was edgy. I thought his testimony was critical to our case. He was a gifted communicator, yet he was ill prepared to recall events and exchanges that had occurred 18 months earlier. Further, I did not like the videotape forum for obtaining his testimony, yet I knew it was the only way we would get him to participate.

At 7:30, the radar still showed no sign of the airplane. My two male colleagues were placidly talking about the upcoming basketball season—who would start, who would excel, and who would disappoint. After their evaluation of the players, they debated the toughness of the schedule and the strengths and weaknesses of our playing facility.

We received a phone call at 7:45 from the third attorney on our team, who was waiting at the deposition site with the plaintiff's lawyers. She said they had restated their complaints about the evening arrangements and were impatient to begin as soon as possible. After the call, my colleagues immediately resumed their conversation by questioning me about the merit and skills of each new freshman on our team.

As the minutes passed, my agitation grew. I knew this was our only chance for testimony from this important witness in our case. Once his season began, he would have no time in his schedule for this bygone affair. In a classic example of misplaced aggression, I seethed at my comrades' calm demeanor and the absolutely irrelevant, inane, time-wasting subjects of their conversation.

At 8:00 p.m., we got the word that the plane was in radar range and would be on the ground in 10 minutes. "This is total bullshit!" I exploded in a rage. "We'll never get this damn thing in tonight and this is our only shot." I paused for air, then erupted again. "This blows our whole case!"

My colleagues were stunned by my outburst. "You just settle down!" one of them said in a scolding tone as if talking to a misbehaving child. "Everything will be fine." His condescension fueled my fury and served to intensify my exasperation.

Fortunately, at that moment, our colleague at the deposition site called to report that our opponents were preparing to leave. They had called the judge to complain about our tardiness and to get permission to reschedule the proceedings. We arrived with our star witness in tow at 8:40 p.m. and promptly called the whole thing off.

For Men

Realize that most women are emotionally expressive and uninhibited. A demonstrative response when you think reticence is appropriate is more likely an indicator of background than true panic. Instead of reading it as hysteria, revel in your gender-related access to emotional self-control.

Bubba Meets Pollyanna

Early in my career in intercollegiate athletics, I decided that eventually I wanted to be an athletics director. I worked on an MBA for 10 years while coaching and doing traditional "women's work" in administration. I knew I would need experience in and around football, men's basketball, and fundraising at some point to have any hope of moving up.

The athletics director at Kentucky gave me that chance in 1993 by offering me the job of fundraiser for our department. My plan was to work in that job for five to seven years and, when my skill set was complete, apply for athletics director positions at smaller schools.

Four-and-a-half years into my tenure as a fundraiser, a job came open in a mid-size Division I university that I thought would be a perfect starting place for me. I called several people I knew, both inside and outside the university, and got the names of those on the search committee. After encouragement from my current boss and a friend on the search committee, I sent in my resume.

After a week, I heard that the committee had received my credentials. Occasionally, I called my friend for an update. She told me it was moving slower than they had hoped and that the president of the university had decided to hire a search firm to assist with the process. She also told me a powerful contingent was favoring someone with a football coaching background, but that she thought from the initial review of applicants that my resume was strong enough to get me an interview.

After several months, I received a letter from the university stating that they had received an open records request from their local newspaper and would be releasing the names of all applicants for the position. A day later, my name appeared in a major paper as one of the finalists for the job.

This public disclosure made me uncomfortable and put me in an awkward position with my donor constituents at home. No one gives money to a fundraiser who is leaving. I called my contact on the search committee for an update. She stunned me by telling me that the president of the search firm had derailed my candidacy, saying my boss had told him I was not ready for the job. This shocked me.

When I asked my boss, he said he had never spoken to anyone from the search firm. I told him that the firm's representative had reported to the internal committee that he lacked confidence in my readiness for the position. Enraged, he called the firm immediately. Fifteen minutes later, he brought me a phone number and told me to call the president of the firm.

Figuring I had no chance at this job anyway, I waited until the position was filled before I called. The search firm president started by telling me that he had secured several $200,000 packages for athletics director clients. He said he dabbles in athletics administration searches because he likes sports, but that he makes his seven-figure salary in private sector searches. This job was small potatoes, he told me. He usually only worked for major institutions. He just took this one to help out a friend.

He then listed the AD searches he had conducted and gave me the details of each compensation package. Regarding several of the appointments, he said, "They owe me for life, I got them such a good deal." At one point, he stated flatly, "It's really all about money." Then, as if realizing someone was on the other end of the phone, he abruptly changed his course. "You need to go to another institution for a couple of years," he stated matter-of-factly. "You need a title with more prestige—associate AD doesn't cut it."

I cut into his monologue to tell him that I had raised more dollars in the past year than the entire budget of the program he had just filled. He cut me off, saying, "It doesn't matter what you do. Get the title "senior associate," then get into every search you can; it won't hurt you as an associate. Sooner or later, you will get a job. It probably won't be a good one, but in two years you can look again."

He glossed over his exchanges with the search committee, saying my friend, who he couldn't remember, had lied about his statements. Then, he patronizingly assured me that I never had a chance at the job anyway.

He ended by asking rhetorically, "You applied for this job, didn't you?" I nodded into the phone. Oblivious to my silence, he rattled on authoritatively, "Never apply for a job, it weakens your candidacy. It devalues you. If you are interested in a position, send me your stuff. In fact, send it to me anyway, certain places are looking for ladies … Have you ever considered working outside of intercollegiate athletics, like at one of the cheerleading organizations or executive director of synchronized swimming?" Again, without waiting for a response, he assured me, "There's money to be made in those organizations. Send me your stuff and I'll find you something and you won't be embarrassed by getting in these searches where you have no chance."

He ended our conversation by asking me to send him a poster of our national championship team. He instructed me to have our men's basketball coach autograph it and write him a personal note on the top.

Our conversation left me shaken. His perspective seemed so valueless. He talked only of money, power, and process. Work and job hunting were competitive events with the score tallied vis-a-vis the size of compensation package, prestige of the institution, and opportunities for further advancement. He never mentioned philosophical compatibility, timeliness of moves, or qualifications.

I felt myself shrinking from the engagement of job hunting. I convinced myself that I could stay in my current position forever and be perfectly contented. I thought I had the "right stuff" to be an athletics director, but suddenly I doubted I had the "balls" to compete for a job.

I realize now that the headhunter was trying to enlist me as a client. In reviewing our conversation, the teaser was the money. He figured that would pique my interest in his services. Then, he used the subtle putdowns to convince me that I needed his help to get a job. His money talk offended me and his criticisms shook my confidence. His intent was to convince me to enter the job hunting fray using him as my agent. He missed his mark. By the time I recognized his motive, I had thrown away his phone number.

For Men

When trying to convince a woman to compete, realize what types of incentives appeal to her achievement motivation. Women generally need to feel confident before they will engage. Remember, for women, acceptance precedes performance. Our confidence is reinforced by a sense of shared values and interpersonal compatibility. The inducements of money, power, and prestige, while they may be important to women, are stronger motivators for men. Value congruity, the likelihood of positive relationships, and personal self-confidence about preparedness are more critical to women's decisions about engagement.

As I mentioned previously, early in my volleyball coaching career, I interviewed for the head job at the University of Notre Dame. I spent most of my interview with the assistant athletics director who would be my direct report. He was a former Notre Dame football player with three daughters who played volleyball. The athletics director joined us for about thirty minutes midway through our session.

I gave the two of them what I thought was a great spiel about intercollegiate athletics, emphasizing academic success, individual development, and personal empowerment. Frequently, I referenced my own experience as a college athlete and my ability to empathize with my players. I discussed my philosophy of coaching and the values gleaned from participation in athletics. The athletics director tired quickly of the idealistic banter. At one point in the conversation, he commented wryly, "At some point, it's all about winning and losing."

I did not get the job. They hired a late-forties male who promised them quick success, national prominence, and positive exposure. Through the grapevine, I learned that they thought I had potential but was too inexperienced for their needs.

They had just finished a disastrous football season and were, at that moment, acutely aware of the zero-sum nature of their business. Looking back, I am sure I sounded like Pollyanna to these battle-hardened administrators. I know now that I interviewed in the wrong mindset. My "group pajama party" approach sounded naive to them. Certainly, they were interested in the merits of participation in intercollegiate athletics, but they knew the job was as much about winning as it was about personal empowerment. My feminized rhetoric about coach/player relationships and individual maturation ignored their perspective. They related better to a candidate that focused on results as opposed to relationships.

For Women

When trying to convince men of your merit or position, make sure you talk in their language. Focus your presentation on bottom-line issues and avoid lengthy elaboration on process and/or interpersonal dynamics. Men want results and are likely to favor someone that says they can deliver them.

What Do I Lose If I Lose?

Several months after C.M. Newton left basketball coaching to accept the position of athletics director at the University of Kentucky, he decided to do a segment on his radio call-in show on the role of coaches' spouses. He invited Carolyn, the spouse of our head football coach; Evelyn, his spouse; and Mark, my spouse.

C.M. and various callers asked the spouses questions about the difficulties of being married to a public figure, the moving that was often part of a coach's life, and their personal reactions to their spouses' successes and failures. All three spouses responded to the first two issues with relatively similar answers, stressing the importance of individual identity and communication between partners in a marriage.

When the discussion turned to the role of the spouse after a loss, their answers were markedly different. Someone asked Carolyn if she ever gave her husband Bill advice about football. She said no, that Bill was the football expert, having studied it his entire career and working with it on a daily basis. She said she had learned a lot about football from him, but would never second-guess his decision-making. Mark admitted, somewhat sheepishly, that the fact that I was the volleyball expert had never stopped him from giving his advice or sharing his opinion about the job I was doing.

A caller asked Evelyn how she interacted with C.M. after a loss. She said her role was to be supportive of him and to let him know that her feelings for him were not based on winning and losing. She pointed out that everyone criticizes a coach after a loss, so they needed support from their families more after a loss than any other time. Mark said he agreed with her position intellectually, but had a hard time responding with support after a loss. His competitiveness made losses so painful for him personally that he frequently joined the critics or simply withdrew to deal with his own disappointment.

These differences in response are easily tied to the worldviews of web and hierarchy. The relationship orientation of the female web places primary value on connections. The results orientation of the male perspective places primary value on accomplishment. The women's instincts were to support and encourage. The man's instincts were to assist and correct. After a loss, the females reacted spontaneously with comfort, the male with judgment.

I appreciated my spouse's honesty in this public forum. It would have been much simpler for him to mimic the women's reactions and present himself as the poster boy for supportive male spouses. Instead, he told the truth: Losing felt very personal to him. His reactions to my failures rotated between rage and discouragement. The women did not judge their spouses' failure with this same mindset. As financial dependents, they were acutely aware of the potential consequences of losses, but their "it's only a game" attitude toward winning and losing kept them from taking ownership of that failure. My husband was not a financial dependent. He had less at stake than his female counterparts. Yet his capacity to show empathy, comfort, and understanding after a loss was limited by his fixation on the calamity of my failure.

For Women

From our perspective, men will overvalue results. They tend to put both wins and losses in a more serious context than we think they deserve. For them, it's not "just a game," it's life. Our feminine instincts to comfort and add perspective will at times be viewed as trivializing the importance of the things they value.

For Men

From your perspective, women will undervalue results. We will put outcomes in the context of play. For us, it is "just a game." Life is about relationships. The masculine instincts to advise and correct will at times be viewed as patronizing and judgmental.

Sink or Swim

In a 1995 book called *Swim with the Dolphins*, authors Connie Glaser and Barbara Steinberg Smalley did a series of interviews with successful women in corporate America. Krys Keller, director of affiliate relations for ABC television, made the following comment in her interview: "… [A]ll of my supervisors have been men, so I've been thrust into a situation of 'sink or swim, pal.'" (8)

Keller's experiences familiarized her with the realities of competing in a predominantly male field. She says about network television: "Women are still outnumbered, and men are still calling the shots … we are playing *their* game on *their* field … ." (9) The male rules dictate that newcomers must fend for themselves before being welcomed, that they must struggle before being accepted, and that they must produce before being granted team membership.

When I was promoted to associate athletics director, I had limited experience in fundraising or human resource management, my two primary areas of responsibility. The athletics director had handpicked me for the job based on his assessment of my potential and to give me a chance to further my career.

He showed me to my new office, introduced me to several men on campus with whom I would interact regularly, and left me to do my job. The files were empty and the predecessor had been gone for a week. I received no instructions, no extra time on the specifics of my job. I was to ask questions if I needed help. My colleagues, while helpful, succinctly answered only the specific questions I asked.

Fortunately, from previous observation, I knew this behavior by the men around me was not a response to my gender. The man who had held the fundraising job before me had been treated the same way. My old office had been across the hall from him and I remember him spending many evenings there when he first arrived. He, also, was left with no files, given no marching orders, and received no coddling or information from his superiors.

He expected none of these. In fact, when the retiring man who had preceded him offered his help, he quickly and aggressively rejected it. My predecessor's background was also limited, but he understood, more clearly than I, the tacit rules of the game. He took pride in figuring out the job on his own. He was keenly attentive to the idiosyncrasies of our corporate culture, and he knew, intuitively, that his ticket to acceptance lay in *his* performance.

I tackled my need for information by quickly learning our computer system so I could search for data on my own. I spent many evenings making connections, studying interactions, and learning relationships. I feigned competence and confidence with both my superiors and subordinates.

Midway through my first year, I landed my first million-dollar donor. Shortly thereafter, the athletics director started telling people publicly that he had always known I would be good at fundraising.

For Women

When entering hierarchical work environments, realize that struggle is part of the rite of passage. Plunge ahead, observe the behavior of your superiors and those of your own rank, fake it until you figure it out, make decisions, take risks. Do not expect feedback, instructions, encouragement, or help. To be accepted and rewarded, you must succeed, initially, on your own.

Early in my administrative career, I hired a young man to help me with event management. He was brand new to the area, but a capable and willing worker. To increase his chances of success, I gave him checklists, met with him regularly, and included him in activities not directly in his purview, but related to our overall organization. I wanted him to feel comfortable with me and others he would be interacting with in our department.

He chafed at my guidance, saying he preferred to develop his own lists and methods, and assuring me that he could handle the tasks I had assigned to him. He rebuffed my attempts to include him in tangential activities, saying he had work to do. It worried me that he never approached me with a problem or question. I knew that his short tenure on the job meant that he was "flying by the seat of his pants" in many situations.

He was a capable young man and became a full-time employee in our department several years later. He has since moved into a managerial role. We became good friends as our careers developed and now talk about our early days together. He shares with me that my attention to him made him feel doubted rather than accepted. He says, "I knew I could do the job and if I screwed it up, I'd hear from you. I didn't appreciate that constant monitoring. Just jump me if I mess up. Otherwise, leave me alone."

We were operating from different playbooks. I wanted him to feel accepted and part of the group, thinking from my female perspective, that this would improve his chances to produce good work. He expected to struggle, to receive little feedback, and to gain acceptance only once he had proved himself. My mothering made him feel doubted rather than supported.

For Men

When entering a web-based work environment, recognize that the advice and assistance offered is an attempt to make you feel part of the group. Your supervisor is not trying to micromanage you and does not distrust your competencies. The sooner you embrace the welcome, the sooner you will be left alone. Rebuff her attempts to make you feel accepted, and she may only try harder.

Avoiding the "Victim" Bear

In the summer of 2001, I was approached by a search firm about my interest in the athletics director's position at a major university. I knew the chancellor from his years at the University of Kentucky. I respected him and was confident I could work with him. The search firm representative told me that their first choice would be a sitting athletics director, but that they wanted to pursue my interest in case they could not hire someone else of their liking.

I was one of four people they decided to interview. The other three were all current athletics directors at Division I programs. I spent a day in meetings with the search committee, the football and men's basketball coaches, and the chancellor. The evening my husband and I returned from the interview, I found out I had moved into the top two. The search committee and coaches were comfortable with either one of us and the chancellor would make a decision the next morning. At 11:00 a.m., the chancellor called and said he had decided to hire the other finalist.

My first exchange after finding out that I had not been selected was with one of our clerks. She said, "They didn't hire you because you're a woman, right?" I said no, the other candidates were all currently ADs and that I thought my lack of head job experience was the main factor in my second-place finish.

I e-mailed my family about the interview and told them I had been nosed out. One responded by pointing out that my sister had been passed over several times for men who were less capable. Sooner or later, the organization had come back to her to bail them out.

A former basketball player and his wife came to my office and asked me whether I was leaving. I told them the school had hired someone else. He said, "Well, you're gonna have a hard time getting a job like that, you being a woman and all."

A colleague in California called on the phone and said, "You got screwed! That guy they hired isn't half the administrator you are. Another case of blatant discrimination."

One of my local supporters said, "I'm glad you're staying here. We're sure lucky you're a woman. If you were a man, someone would have hired you away a long time ago."

I know all these people were trying to make me feel better about losing the job. After all, if it was gender discrimination, then I was blameless. They were excusing me from any responsibility to improve my performance in future interviews, to get more training, or to grow my circle of connections.

Each time I heard their comments, I could feel the victim bear jumping on my back, that invisible weight that whispers fiendishly in your ear, "It's gender, stupid. You got no chance, not now, not ever. Forget it." Their well-intentioned consolations were in effect invitations to despair.

The exchanges reminded me of a conversation I had listened to several years before. I had attended a lecture on black women in sport given by Sonja Steptoe, a CNN/SI national correspondent, and one of only a handful of African American women in sports journalism.

Following her remarks, a white male in the audience asked her, "Do you feel you have to be much better than your male counterparts to succeed?"

She answered without hesitation, "In general, 'no'—just when I don't feel like rewriting something that my editor tells me to rewrite or do another interview that I don't want to do. But, in general, 'no.' Sometimes, I even get better assignments because of what I bring to the table, my perspective and credentials."

The questioner persisted, saying, "Doesn't the very lack [of African American women in sports journalism] say something though?"

Steptoe replied, "Maybe, maybe not. I think you have to be careful about drawing conclusions based on sheer numbers … These jobs are hard; I travel all the time, I'm single … You can't be married and have children and do the job that I do … For a lot of women, [investigative reporting] is distasteful … My life is not my own … These are the reasons a lot of women don't want to do this stuff."

Catching herself sounding self-pitying, she said, "It's a great gig, don't get me wrong. I feel privileged to have it … I am the beneficiary of affirmative action and look at where I've gotten … I think the opportunities are there … If you are really good and a hard worker, eventually it shows up and people recognize it." (10)

I found her answer refreshing and affirming. She refused to be stereotyped, rejecting the premise that her lot was singularly difficult. To her way of thinking, she was neither a victim nor a hero. She had traded marriage and children for a front-row seat and national notoriety at high-profile sporting events—a no-brainer for a lot of men, an unsatisfying choice for a lot of women. She had sacrificed relationships for fulfilling work—a choice traditionally made more often by men than women. She was unapologetic about her choices, modestly reveling in her accomplishments. Yet she was equally unsympathetic to those coveting her job but unwilling to make the same choices.

Whatever the connection between us, her words encouraged me. Maybe we shared situations—both in historically male occupations, both childless. Maybe we were at the same stages in our careers—established but still climbing, fulfilled but still questioning. Maybe we were just both fighting to keep the victim bear off our backs and out of our thinking.

For Women

Sometimes, well-meaning people will give you an excuse to fail. Turn it down. No one can make you a victim. You must agree to it.

For Men

Beware of the victim bear. Now that you must compete with women for jobs and promotions, don't let the bear catch you.

Epilogue

I had the good fortune to work for a man who modeled for me a unique leadership style. In 1989, C.M. Newton was hired as the director of athletics at the University of Kentucky. He took over a department shaken to its very core. Serious rules violations, unethical conduct, the forced resignation of the former athletics director, and the financial uncertainty of sanctions had people in the department and across the Commonwealth feeling wary, disheartened, embarrassed, and angry.

Early in his tenure, I accompanied him to a banquet in Louisville. C.M. was receiving an award, so he sat at the head table. I sat in the audience next to Ralph Beard, a former Kentucky basketball great and C.M.'s teammate on our 1949 National Championship basketball team.

During dinner, Ralph said to me, "Kathy, let me tell you something. C.M. Newton is the perfect choice for our athletics director and I'll tell you why—he has the heart of a woman and the strength of a man, and we desperately need both of those right now." Ralph understood the fragile nature of our situation and that management of it would require both love and fortitude.

The meaning of Ralph's remark was not immediately apparent to me. I did not know C.M. well at the time and had never worked with him. However, the interesting imagery of the phrase stuck with me. I remembered it several years later as I was pondering the issues in this book. I realized that in that one simple phrase—*the heart of a woman and the strength of a man*— Ralph had identified the quality that made C.M. Newton a distinctively gifted leader.

In the 11 years I worked with him, he taught me many ways to mesh heart and strength. He favored building partnerships rather than negotiating business deals, even if that meant leaving money on the table. He showed me how to use intuition when hiring, compassion when firing, and directness when disciplining. He modeled detached control when I knew his heart was breaking, and remarkable restraint when he was intentionally wronged. The androgynous blend of male and female traits is what I admired most about C.M. I adopted Ralph's phrase as a secret mantra. I dreamed that one day, someone would say it about me.

During my lengthy internal debate about my own gender identity, I had visited the polar ends of the heart/strength spectrum. I had observed both extremes in play and work situations. I found in myself and others that when we obsessed with strength, we never questioned the value of winning, assuming it was always worth the sacrifice. Likewise, when we obsessed with heart, we vilified winning, certain it was never worth the sacrifice. Neither is correct.

Our challenge is to find our own personal balance of heart and strength. No generic road map exists. We must each choose when to be silent and when to protest, when to acquiesce and when to overpower, when to manipulate and when to strong-arm. But if we can lead with both compassion and courage, and follow with both conscience and conviction, we can shape a new paradigm for effectiveness in a pluralistic society.

Notes

Published or broadcast sources of information are cited in these notes. Where none is cited, the author's source was a personal interview, conversation, or recollection.

Chapter 1

1. Hall, Mike, *Albuquerque Journal*, Saturday, January 20, 2001, D1-2.

2. Gilligan, Carol, *In A Different Voice: Psychological Theory and Women's Development* (Cambridge, Massachusetts: Harvard University Press, 1982)

3. Tannen, Deborah, *You Just Don't Understand: Men and Women in Conversation* (New York: William Morrow and Company, Inc., 1990)

4. Keen, Sam, *Fire in the Belly: A Book about Men* (New York: Bantam Books, 1991)

5. Gray, John, *Men Are From Mars, Women Are From Venus* (New York: HarperCollins Publishers, 1992)

6. Kerr, Barbara, *Smart Girls, Gifted Women* (Dayton: Ohio Psychology Press, 1985)

7. Peters, Tom, *USA Today*, February 27, 1998, 8B.

8. Lerner, Harriet Goldhor, *The Dance of Deception* (New York: HarperCollins Publishing, 1994) 6.

9. Chodorow, Nancy, "Family Structure and Feminine Personality." M.Z Rosaldo and L. Lamphere, eds., Woman, Culture and Society (Stanford: Stanford University Press, 1974) 43.

    Chodorow, Nancy, *The Reproduction of Mothering* (Berkeley: University of California Press, 1978)

10. Price, S.L., "Anson Dorrance," *Sports Illustrated*, December 7, 1998, 100.

11. Gilligan, Carol, *In A Different Voice: Psychological Theory and Women's Development* (Cambridge, Massachusetts: Harvard University Press, 1982) 62.

12. Tannen, Deborah, *You Just Don't Understand: Men and Women in Conversation* (New York: William Morrow and Company, Inc. 1990) 24-25.

13. Ibid, 24-25

14. Belenky, M.F. et. al., *Women's Ways of Knowing* (New York: HarperCollinsPublishers, Inc., 1986) 102.

15. Kerr, Barbara, *Smart Girls, Gifted Women* (Dayton: Ohio Psychology Press, 1985) 101.

16. Branta, C.F. et.al. "Gender Differences in play patterns and sport participation of North American Youth." D. Gould and M.R. Weiss, eds., *Advances in Pediatric Sport Sciences* Vol. 2 (Champaign: Human Kinetics Publishers, 1987)

17. Gray, John, *Men Are From Mars, Women Are From Venus* (New York: HarperCollinsPublishers, 1992) 48.

18. Ibid, 44.

19. Valentine, John, Ph.D. "What Do Men Have to Offer?" Unpublished paper, 1985.

20. Kerr, Barbara, *Smart Girls, Gifted Women* (Dayton: Ohio Psychology Press, 1985) 140.

21. bid, 140-141.

Chapter 2

1. *U.S. News & World Report*, June 15, 1998, 14.

2. Huntington, Anna Seaton, *New York Times*, May 17, 1998, SP 11.

3. *Lexington Herald-Leader*, May 20, 1997

4. Horner, Matina, "Toward an Understanding of Achievement-Related Conflicts in Women." Journal of Social Issues, 1972, 28, 157-175.

5. Nelson, Mariah Burton, *Embracing Victory* (New York: William Morrow and Company, Inc., 1998) 58.

6. Heim, Pat, *Hardball for Women: Winning at the Game of Business*, New York: Penguin Books, USA, Inc., 1992) 85.

7. Ibid, 48.

8. Ibid, 52.

9. Ibid, 72-73.

10. Price, S.L., "Anson Dorrance," *Sports Illustrated*, Vol. 89, No. 23, December 7, 1998, 88.

11. Heim, Pat, *Hardball for Women*, 79.

12. Huntington, Anna Seaton, *Making Waves: The Inside Story of Managing and Motivating the First Women's Team to Compete for the America's Cup* (Texas: The Summit Publishing Group, 1996) 115-116.

13. Ibid, 122.

14. Ibid, 116.

15. Ibid, 113-128.

16. Ibid, xvi.

17. Dorrance, Anson with Tim Nash, *Training Soccer Champions* (North Carolina: JTC Sports, Inc., 1996) 65.

18. DeBoer, Kathleen J., "What do I win if I win?" Interscholastic Athletic Administration, Vol. 25, Number 3, Spring, 1999, 10-15.

19. Dorrance, *Training Soccer Champions*, 66.

Chapter 3

1. Roberts, Cokie, "Like Mother, Like Daughter," *LIFE*, May 1999, 46.

2. Shellenbarger, Sue, "Men, women more alike study shows," *The Detroit News*, April 19, C 1.

3. Bellafonte, Gina, "Feminism: It's all about me!" *Time*, Vol. 151, No. 25, 58.

4. Fisher, Helen, *The First Sex* (New York: Random House Inc., 1999) xvi-xvii.

5. Ibid, 106.

6. McKenna, Elizabeth Perle, *When Work Doesn't Work Anymore* (New York: Bantam Doubleday Dell Publishing Group, 1997) 54.

7. Printed in *Coaching Volleyball*, Vol. II, No. 5, June/July 1989, 24-27.

8. McKenna, Elizabeth Perle, *When Work Doesn't Work Anymore* (New York: Bantam Doubleday Dell Publishing Group, 1997) 51.

9. Dorrance, Anson with Tim Nash, *Training Soccer Champions* (North Carolina: JTC Sports, Inc. 1996) 64.

10. Smith, Gary "The Wizard of Knoxville," *Sports Illustrated*, March 2, 1998, 97.

11. *When Work Doesn't Work Anymore* (New York: Bantam Doubleday Dell Publishing Group, Inc., 1997) 150.

12. Sellers, Patricia, "Women, Sex, and Power," *Fortune*, August 5, 1996, 53.

13. Heim, Patricia, *Hardball for Women: Winning at the Game of Business* (New York: Penguin Books, USA, Inc., 1992) 85.

14. VanDerveer, Tara, *Shooting from the Outside* (New York, New York: Avon Books, 1997) 32-33.

15. Gibbs, Nancy, "The Many Lives of Madeleine," *TIME*, February 17, 1997, 56, 58, 61.

16. Heim, Patricia, *Hardball for Women*, 124.

17. Saffo, Paul, Interview with *Bottom Line*, August 1, 1996.

18. Peters, Tom, LIVE, audio tape of presentation, 1991.

Chapter 4

1. Tifft, Susan E., "Board Gains: Women Start to Win a Place at the Table," *Working Woman*, 19:2 (1994), 36.

2. *Chronicle on Higher Education*, Fall 1999.

3. Janice, Elizabeth E., "The Male-Female Wage Gap," *1995 Information Please Business Almanac and Source*, Boston: Houghton Mifflin Co., 1994.

4. Arnett, A.C., "Futurists Gaze into Business's Crystal Ball," The Washington Post, July 20, 1989, F1-F2.

5. Gray, John, *Men are from Mars, Women are from Venus* (New York, New York: Harper Collins Publishers, 1992) 29.

6. Ibid, 17.

7. Jamieson, Kathleen Hall, *Beyond the Double Bind* (New York: Oxford University Press, 1995) 95.

8. Glaser, Connie and Barbara Steinberg Smalley, *Swim with the Dolphins* (New York, New York: Warner Books, Inc., 1998) 257.

9. Ibid, 255.

10. Steptoe, Sonja, Transcribed from video of lecture, Friday, October 23, 1998, Student Center Theater, University of Kentucky. Permission to quote given by Ms. Steptoe Dec. 4, 1998.

Suggested Readings

Belenky, M.F. et. al., Women's Ways of Knowing (New York: Harper Collins Publishers, Inc., 1986)

DeBoer, Kathleen J., "Growing Up Female and Athlete," *Coaching Women's Basketball*, February/March, 1991, Vol. 5, No. 3, 9-11, 29-30

————, "Optimizing Performance in Team Sport Women Athletes," *Coaching Volleyball*, February/March, 1998, 22-27

————, "How to Improve the Competitiveness of Female Teams" *Women in Higher Education*, February 2001, Vol. 10, No. 2, 7-8

Dorrance, Anson with Tim Nash, *Training Soccer Champions* (North Carolina: JTC Sports, Inc. 1996)

Epperson, David Canning, *A Woman's Touch: What Today's Women Can Teach Us About Sport and Life* (South Bend, IN: Diamond Communications, Inc., 1999)

Estrich, Susan, *Sex & Power* (New York, New York: Riverhead Books, 2000)

Evans, Gail, *Play Like a Man Win Like a Woman*, (New York, New York: Broadway Books, Inc., 2000)

Fisher, Helen, *The First Sex* (New York: Random House Inc., 1999)

Glaser, Connie and Barbara Steinberg Smalley, *Swim with the Dolphins* (New York, New York: Warner Books, Inc., 1998)

Gray, John, *Men are from Mars, Women are from Venus* (New York, New York: Harper Collins Publishers, 1992)

Gilligan, Carol, *In A Different Voice: Psychological Theory and Women's Development* (Cambridge, Massachusetts: Harvard University Press, 1982)

Graham, Katherine, *Personal History* (New York: Alfred A. Knopf, Inc., 1997)

Harrigan, Betty Lehan, Games Mother Never Taught You, (New York, New York: Warner Books, Inc., 1992)

Heim, Pat, *Hardball for Women: Winning at the Game of Business* (New York: Penguin Books, USA, Inc., 1992)

Huntington, Anna Seaton, *Making Waves: The Inside Story of Managing and Motivating the First Women's Team to Compete for the America's Cup* (Texas: The Summit Publishing Group, 1996)

Jamieson, Kathleen Hall, *Beyond the Double Bind*, (New York: Oxford University Press, 1995)

Keen, Sam, *Fire in the Belly: A Book about Men* (New York: Bantam Books, 1991)

Kerr, Barbara, *Smart Girls, Gifted Women* (Dayton: Ohio Psychology Press, 1985)

Lerner, Harriet Goldhor, *The Dance of Deception* (New York: HarperCollins Publishing, 1994)

McKenna, Elizabeth Perle, *When Work Doesn't Work Anymore* (New York: Bantam Doubleday Dell Publishing Group, 1997)

Mendell, Adrienne, *How Men Think* (New York: Fawcett Columbine, 1996)

Mindell, Phyllis, *A Woman's Guide to the Language of Success* (Paramus, NJ: Prentice Hall, 1995)

Nelson, Mariah Burton, *Embracing Victory* (New York: William Morrow and Company, Inc., 1998)

Popcorn, Faith, and Lys Marigold, *EVEolution: The Eight Truths of Marketing to Women* (New York: Hyperion, 2000)

Price, S.L., "Anson Dorrance," *Sports Illustrated*, December 7, 1998, 86-103.

Rimm, Sylvia et. al. How Jane Won: 55 Successful Women Share How They Grew from Ordinary Girls to Extraordinary Women (New York: Crown Publishers, 2001)

——. *See Jane Win: The Rimm Report on How 1,000 Girls Became Successful Women* (New York: Three Rivers Press, 1999)

Rubin, Harriet, *The Princessa: Machiavelli for Women* (New York: Bantam Doubleday Dell Publishing Group, Inc., 1997)

Smith, Gary "The Wizard of Knoxville," *Sports Illustrated*, March 2, 1998, 88-104

Stahl, Lesley, *Reporting Live* (New York: Touchstone, 1999)

Steinem, Gloria, *Revolution from Within* (Boston: Little, Brown and Company, 1992)

Tannen, Deborah, *You Just Don't Understand: Men and Women in Conversation* (New York: William Morrow and Company, Inc. 1990)

VanDerveer, Tara, *Shooting from the Outside*, (New York, New York: Avon Books, 1997)

Zuker, Elaina, *The Seven Secrets of Influence* (New York: McGraw-Hill, Inc. 1991)

About the Author

Kathleen DeBoer is the commissioner of general services for the Lexington-Fayette Urban County Government, a position she assumed in January 2003. Prior to that, she was the senior associate athletics director at the University of Kentucky.

DeBoer has worked in and around athletics all of her life. One of the first women offered a college athletics scholarship at Michigan State University, she went on to play professional basketball in the WBL, one of the first women's leagues.

Following her playing career, she was a successful collegiate coach at Ferris State University and the University of Kentucky, earning National Coach of the Year honors in 1987.

DeBoer served as an advisor to the USA National Team from 1988 to 1996 and assisted with the 1996 Olympic Volleyball Team. She was a member of the NCAA Management Council and served for 10 years as the chief fund raising officer of the University of Kentucky Athletics Association.

The author of numerous articles and videotapes on the subjects of gender, competition, and coaching, DeBoer is a sought-after speaker for groups as diverse as athletics administrators, women in law enforcement, and high school students. She also is a frequent keynote speaker at academic conferences and business seminars.

She is married to Mark Pittman and resides in Lexington, Kentucky.